BILL JASON PRIEST
Community College Pioneer

Bill Jason Priest

Community College Pioneer

Kathleen Krebbs Whitson

Foreword by
Edmund J. Gleazer

University of
North Texas Press
Denton, Texas

The paper in this book meets the minimum requirements of the
American National Standard for Permanence of Paper for Printed
Library Materials, Z39.48.1984

Permissions
University of North Texas Press
PO Box 311336
Denton, TX 76203-1336
940-565-2142

Library of Congress Cataloging-in-Publication Data
Whitson, Kathleen Krebbs, 1947-
    Bill Jason Priest, community college pioneer / Kathleen Krebbs
Whitson ; foreword by Edmund J. Gleazer.— 1st ed.
        p. cm.
Includes bibliographical references and index.
    ISBN 1-57441-174-8 (cloth : alk. paper)
    1. Priest, Bill Jason, 1917- 2. Community college administrators—
Texas—Dallas County—Biography. 3. Dallas County Community
College District. I. Title.
LA2317.P74W45 2004
370'.92—dc22
                                        2003019705

Design by Angela Schmitt

Photo gallery made possible by a generous grant from the
Buchholz Family Foundation.

Dedication

To my husband who has forever been my encourager, my compass, my best friend, and, on occasion, my thesaurus.

Contents

List of Illustrations following page 68:

1. Adah Freeman Stubbs, Bill Priest's grandmother, in the early 1900s
2. Four-year old Bill Priest
3. Bill Priest on Berkeley campus in the spring of 1935
4. Promotional photograph of Bill Priest as Berkeley baseball pitcher
5. Promotional photograph of Bill Priest as member of Philadelphia Athletics ball club
6. Bill Priest (left) in Mindanao, Philippines during World War II
7. Bill Priest (left) in front of the Manila Hotel
8. Bill Priest struck a pose with a cigar imitating Winston Churchill
9. First of many official portraits of Bill Priest, Dallas, 1965
10. First board of trustees the Dallas County Community College District and Chancellor Priest
11. Sanger Brothers Department Store building, renovated to house El Centro College, 1966
12. El Centro employees exaggerated lack of safety in staff offices
13. Bill Priest accepts a scholarship check for Dallas County Junior College students, circa 1969
14. Eastfield College, 1970
15. Mountain View College
16. Mountain View College landscape
17. Richland College
18. Northlake College, 1977
19. Cedar Valley College
20. Cedar Valley College landscape
21. Cedar Valley College dedication ceremony
22. Brookhaven College and infamous windmill
23. Marietta and Bill Priest with Carol Schlipak
24. Priest delivers speech at the national AACJC convention
25. The lead instructor in the El Centro Culinary Arts Degree program Gus Katsigris with Priest
26. Priest, 1988, on a fishing trip in Alaska
27. In 1991, Priest hunts in Alberta, Canada
28. Bill and Ann Priest, 1997
29. Priest addresses 1999 League for Innovation Conference
30. DCCCD chancellors
31. DCCCD chancellor, Jesus Carreon, 2003

Foreword

This is the story of the remarkable development of a new kind of educational institution, through the experiences of Bill J. Priest, a maverick who took the reins in building for Dallas what Bob Thornton called the "the best damn junior college in the country."

I enjoyed this book. There is nothing dry or abstract about it. Is the story well told? It is. I have known Bill since we first came together on the junior college front in the late 1940s. I thought I knew a lot about him, but the book revealed much that he did not share easily with even his closest friends but has shaped his life and leadership style. It is fascinating to become aware of personal struggles and fortuitous happenings usually hidden beneath the title and the public persona of community college president. Read and discover how the bow tie, the vigorous competitive drive, and the disdain for incompetence played out in building an institution from a concept to seven colleges, each to serve ten-thousand students.

Although the focus is on Bill Priest the story is bigger than a person. In the 1960s, the unprecedented establishment of five-hundred community colleges opened in this country. In twenty of our major cities, including Cleveland, Miami, St. Louis, and Dallas, we would see "peoples colleges"—low cost, close to home, and with open admissions. Great numbers of unimaginably diverse people entered these new doors of opportunity. To make this possible, often contending governmental entities needed to be brought together in partnership, and citizens had to be convinced to vote for new districts, and to make the necessary tax funds available for facilities and operating costs. The institutions adapted to meet the needs of often unconventional college students. And they must have been successful because in almost every case enrollments increased beyond expectations.

This decade of educational ferment in the United States deserves more attention by historians than it has yet been given. The story of Bill Priest and the Dallas County Community College District is a lively and engrossing report within the bigger picture.   Those professionals now entering or preparing to enter the field in great numbers can benefit from the experience of these community college pioneers as they shaped the modern comprehensive community college. And Dallas County Community College—under the leadership of the right man, in the right place, at the right time—led the way.

Edmund J. Gleazer

Preface

As people began to learn that I was planning to write the biography of Bill Priest, the responses were expressions of surprise followed by comments of approval. Several added that they could not believe someone had not already done this. Those reactions assured me that my own sense of the importance of this project was shared by others, including not only long-time employees in the Dallas County Community College District (DCCCD), but also national leaders in higher education.

My interest in writing about Priest first came about as I attended a seminar while working on my doctorate in higher education at the University of North Texas. Conducted by Professor Barry Lumsden, the seminar focused on the perils and profits of writing a dissertation. I had a topic, a theory base, and a proposal draft that had the approval of my major professor, Howard Smith. As I researched, the topic began to grow and the dissertation seemed to take on a life of its own. I felt overwhelmed and thought I would be graduating in my dotage.

During Lumsden's discussion of historical studies, the idea revealed itself. Historical research appealed to me because it has a beginning and an end. It goes without saying that I wanted the topic to be significant enough to be worthy of graduate level work. I thought of Bill Priest, founder of the Dallas County Community College District, where I had invested much of my work life. I knew his impact on the community college movement had been more than the founding of the Dallas district. My third motivation was that I would get to interview Priest. I loved to hear him talk. As a communications major, I was fascinated by his variegated use of language and unique verbal imagery.

In my initial research and review of the literature to write my proposal, I was surprised and delighted to learn of the number of programs and services that Priest had pioneered and/or helped to evolve into national usage. The importance of the community college in higher education loomed large in the literature, and the man on whom I had chosen to focus my research was a major player. This dissertation proved to be a labor of love. I enjoyed meeting or getting to know better other community college leaders my subject required me to interview. It was a special pleasure interviewing Margaret McDermott, who invited me to her home for lunch. Seeing all of the original paintings by renowned artists was an enriching experience. She was gracious and accommodating and I could see why she had been selected to serve on the founding board of trustees and why she and Priest had become friends. She told me how pleased she was that I had chosen Bill Priest for my dissertation research. As a result of my dissertation research, I learned considerably about the DCCCD, and the people who had brought it to life. This was in addition to all I learned about the contributions of Priest and the evolution of junior colleges to comprehensive community colleges.

Writing, of course, is not a one time event. It involves a series of outlines, drafts, rewrites, and more rewrites. At one iteration of my dissertation review by committee, the professor from the University at large, not from my major or minor area, put a red circle around "Bill" each time I had written it in the copy. Also in red at the top of the front page with an arrow pointing to "Bill," he wrote, "Isn't this a little informal for a scholarly work?" I explained to him that it was not informal; it was indeed Priest's given name, not William. In fact, it is a most appropriate name. Bill is Bill. It is an all American down-home name lacking in airs, which is exactly who Priest is. He doesn't know why his parents chose to name him simply "Bill," but without a doubt it is befitting the man he came to be.

The dissertation evolved to an acceptable level and passed the defense. It was well received and has been read by more than just the University doctoral committee. The fact that others outside those who were required to read my dissertation chose to read it, made me feel affirmed in the selection of my topic and the value of the study. Even so, the readership would be only a few. I frequently heard younger employees in the Dallas County Community College District respond to the mention of Bill Priest with, "You mean the Institute for Economic Development?" They didn't know about the man who had given them a place to work.

The full dimension of Priest's part in the development of the DCCCD was recorded in my dissertation. In fact, various aspects of the district had been the topic of several other dissertations. By their nature, dissertations are dry, redundant, and not widely read except by other researchers. To increase the readership and bring more public awareness to the contributions of Priest in the community college movement, a published book was needed. The recommendation of the publisher was a biography with more personal descriptions. Fortunately, Priest is a unique person, not the stereotypical college president of dark suits, white shirts, holed up in an office of heavy mahogany furniture, who comes forth only for special occasions to give academically astute sounding speeches. Priest lives life as a great adventure. He has an abiding passion for education. Above all, he is always himself in all settings. Priest, the man, would lend flavor to a book on Priest, the educator.

This book was written from many interviews with Priest, himself, and those who know him personally and professionally, and from early documents, published articles, and previous research. The bulk of the research was completed at the dissertation stage, but additional interviews and research were done to enliven the book with information inappropriate for a dissertation. There was a certain amount written from personal memories. I began working in the DCCCD in January 1977 and was present at many of the events discussed by others in their interviews and have watched the growth and changes from then until now. Documents, photographs, and the memories of the people who were there form the data for historical research. The critics of historical research cite it as being subjective and limited by the human perspective. Those elements are part of every discipline other than math or science, and there is some argument to support a certain amount of subjectivity even in those.

There are two levels of historical research. One is the recording of the facts, simply telling what happened. The second is the substance of what happened, the short and long range effects. History is more than a chronology of events. It is the influence on the people who lived it and their influence on the subsequent years. There is particular value in historical research in the field of education. It provides increased understanding on how the educational process has evolved to this point, which serves as a basis for further progress. Educators are entwined with the present and the past while trying to navigate through trends and fads in order to discern true strategic directions for the future. The study of the history of education assists those in the field to evaluate lasting contributions, and to distinguish them from momentary successes. With the retirement of long-time employees, each institution loses part of its unrecorded history. A biography draws deeply from both aspects of history, the recorded facts and the community of memories. This book focuses on the past of the comprehensive community college in higher education through the life of Bill Priest. With the graying of the campuses and the many numbers of faculty members, administrators, and staff queued for retirement, preserving this history in an accessible form is essential.

CHAPTER ONE

Early Influences

B ill Priest stood chuckling as the more than seven hundred people who had gathered to honor him laughed and applauded. The occasion was his retirement from the Dallas County Community College District (DCCCD) after fifteen years as chancellor. A group of college administrators and faculty gathered around him on stage bedecked in t-shirts ablaze with red letters declaring: "Priest, a legend in his own time." They ceremoniously presented him with a t-shirt imprinted, "A Legend in his own Mind." Everyone, including Bill Priest, enjoyed the humor of the pun, but everyone, with the exception of Priest, knew he was a legend in the world of community colleges. He was a leader among leaders in two-year higher education and had founded a college district in one of the largest cities in Texas, a district he developed into a national model for other community colleges. This was the surprising career legacy of a young lad from a small rural town in California, whose lineage consisted of farmers, religious leaders, and sportsmen.

In 1917, Woodrow Wilson was president and the United States had just entered World War I by declaring war on Germany. The

Chicago White Sox won the World Series by beating the New York Yankees four out of six games. The population of the United States was just over one-hundred-million with fifty percent settled in rural homesteads. William D. Stephens was in his first year as governor of California and the state legislature passed a law providing funding for public junior colleges. On September 23, 1917, in rural French Camp, California, Bill Jason was born to Jesse and Clarice Priest. To describe 1917 French Camp as rural is an embellishment. The tiny town had been founded in the pre-gold rush days of 1828 as a beaver trapping post and it had not developed much beyond that. The Priests already had one child, a three-and-a-half year old daughter, Maradah. The family lived in a poorly constructed shack and Jesse tried to farm the unfertile land around it. Jesse and Clarice had each been eighteen years old when they married in 1912. Neither had graduated from high school.

Jesse was the adopted son of Will and Mary Priest. Fortunately, most of the Priest family had escaped the country's flu epidemic of 1918, but in 1919, Jesse's mother died from cancer. Medical treatment in the early 1900s was not easily accessible to Mary Priest, nor was it of much value when dealing with catastrophic illnesses. After his mother's death, Jesse moved his wife and two children from their less than adequate dwelling to live with his father in an eighteen-room house on a four-hundred acre ranch just outside Stockton, California. That move brought together opportunities and conflicts which greatly influenced the young Bill Priest through his formative years.

Jesse Priest's father was an elder in the First Christian Church and had aspirations for his son to become a preacher. Jesse not only rejected the notion of making his living preaching, but also took issue with all formalized religion. Bill Priest grew up attending the First Christian Church with his paternal grandfather part of the time and attending the Unity Church with his maternal grandmother, Adah Freeman Stubbs, other times. In between, he heard in-home sermons of religious refutation from his father and bellowing arguments between his father and his grandfather. He also observed his soft-hearted grandfather being taken advantage of by glib-tongued fellows tapping him for monetary support of various religious causes. One such young man duped him twice. The first time he claimed to be an evangelist in need of land on which to erect a building for a school of theology. With all good faith, Priest's grandfather gave him the deeds to pieces of land only to have the swindler slip into the night with cash in hand. The same man returned some time later with a new scheme, Priest's grandfather complied with the request for money, and again, no religious good came of it. While his grandfather seemed to forgive and forget, Priest never forgot and developed a wary view of formalized religion. Priest did not throw out the grain with the organized religious chaff and gleaned from its moral teachings a philosophy of forthrightness that would serve him well throughout his life. He also developed a conservative concept of all issues being either black or white with no shades of gray, which would put him at odds with others, and occasionally, even himself.

One of the eighteen rooms of his boyhood home housed the library of James Budd, who had been the governor of California from 1895 to 1899. Governor Budd had bequeathed the library to Priest's great aunt, Dr. Clara Freeman. Dr. Freeman was a medical doctor, an unusual profession for a woman in the early 1900s. Priest's mother, being the favorite niece, had inherited the library from her aunt. In 1897, Governor Budd signed legislation authorizing the establishment of San Diego Normal School to produce teachers for the city's growing population. Like foreshadowing in a Charles Dickens' novel, Priest's young mind was fed from the library of a political advocate for education.

A prolific reader from a very early age, Priest developed a love of history and by the age of seven, had a clear focus on what he wanted to be when he grew up—a history teacher. Unlike most seven-year- old children who dream of being cowboys and firemen, Priest's eye was on teaching. His other talents, and intervening events, would however, not allow his career path to be direct to this clearly defined goal.

He glided unchallenged through the first four grades, and was double promoted to the sixth grade, skipping the fifth. Even with that advancement, his teacher had to create a special reading class just for him. He was given books on an advanced level and left to read on his own.

The grammar school was located in French Camp, California, whose student population was fifty percent Japanese. This first-hand cultural experience was quite unusual for Anglo children in the 1920s, and was in this case due in part to Priest's family. His grandfather had sold ten acres of his ranch to Japanese immigrants. The parcel of land was fertile loam and from this successful farmland grew a Japanese settlement. This experience enriched Priest's education and broadened his cultural awareness. Eighth grade graduation completed grammar school.

In high school he noticed a beautiful girl, one he had also seen horseback riding past his home. She was two grades ahead of him, and that seemed like a chasm. He did not approach her.

Priest's high school days were not the same educational experience for him as had been grammar school. There were no real problems in the ninth grade, but by the tenth he was hit by a series of events that drained the motivation from him and left him wondering about what was really important in life.

Priest's father was given to drink and like most alcoholics, inebriation brought out his worst characteristics. As a boy, Priest relied more on his mother for parenting and was exceptionally close to his grandmother. That school year, his mother became critically ill and was hospitalized. One day, someone came to get him because his mother was near death. When Priest arrived at the hospital, his father was there, but was drunk. Priest seethed with anger, feeling his mother was being betrayed in her final hours. She recovered, but as a boy of fourteen, Priest had no forgiveness for his father's self-indulgence at the time of his mother's need.

Following this incident, Priest lost his sanctuary. His maternal grandmother, Adah Freeman Stubbs, died. He had been very close to her and deeply admired her intelligence and resilience. A child of the mountains, she migrated with her family to California in an ox cart in 1858. She grew up, by virtue of necessity, as a naturalist, and developed remarkable skills of survival. She read the signs of nature to forecast the weather and could make meals from the vegetation around her cabin. She could make new tools from what was left of something broken or worn out. She lived by the principle that if you want it done, you do it yourself. But she was not her own focus; she always thought of others first. Priest was fascinated by her abilities and independent spirit. He spent many days with her while he was growing up and he was her favorite grandchild.

Her death was not kind or swift. A strep infection caused her to slowly deteriorate and then lie in a coma for ten days before succumbing to the illness. Watching the strong woman he admired growing weaker and withering before dying was more than Priest could emotionally process. To him, the loss of such a remarkable and special person made all else seem meaningless.

Another comfort to Priest was the close relationship he had with his sister, but that same year she married and moved away. This was joy mixed with sorrow for the young Priest. He was happy for his sister, but again for him it was a loss of personal support, an important and reachable relationship. In his sophomore year, the star of French Camp Grammar School made two C's and two D's at Stockton High School.

But the pendulum of life swings wide in opposite directions. That same year, one of the most positive events of his life also occurred. Harold Vogelsang, the Chief of Police, filled many roles in Stockton. One was coach of Stockton's Karl Ross American Legion Junior Baseball team. The rules of the league included an age limit of seventeen, and Vogelsang's team lost eleven players that year due to the rule. In seeking new talent, he encouraged Priest to try out. Priest had not played baseball in school because the Stockton high school did not have a baseball team, but he had the skills of a seasoned player. His father had played pro ball as a catcher in the Three I league, and young Priest had learned to pitch under his tutelage. Priest was quite adept at throwing a curve ball, a distinct advantage in the junior world of baseball. In 1932, at the age of fourteen, Priest became the first string pitcher for Stockton's American Legion team.

The team did very well. In 1933, winning state and regional championships took them to Topeka, Kansas for the sectional title series. They were eliminated by the Chicago American Legion team in the national semi-finals. It was a disappointing loss, but the team from the little town of Stockton, California had attained significant success at the national level and had much of which to be proud.

As a reward for the team, and a great educational opportunity, Coach Vogelsang took them to Chicago to attend the World's Fair, Century of Progress. The boys were amazed by the impressive cornucopia of exhibits, but nothing was as exciting to the ball club as going to a Chicago White Sox game. Being a spectator at a professional major league baseball game was a first for Priest. The White Sox beat the Philadelphia Athletics eleven to five with cheers and applause from the Stockton American Legion team members, not so much for one side or the other, but from sheer joy.

Before the game, Priest met and shook the hand of Kenesaw Mountain Landis, the first commissioner of baseball. Also an American jurist, Judge Landis served as commissioner from 1921 to 1944. He helped to restore the American public's faith in baseball after the "Black Sox" scandal of 1919. For Priest, meeting baseball's top person was "like going to baseball heaven." In truth, the meeting in Chicago was little more than a junior baseball player from a small town having a special opportunity to tour the big city and mingle with the professionals in the sport of his passion. It would, however, prove to be more significant in just a few years as Priest's career would take him to one of the teams under the watchful eye of Judge Landis.

The success of the young Stockton baseball team brought a bit of notoriety to all its members and Priest became known in the community. With his competitive nature and desire not to disappoint those who placed faith in him, being in the spotlight made him want to do well in all aspects of his life. He refocused his efforts in high school, and his grades improved dramatically. He returned to the level of academic achievement in line with his abilities by earning four A's and one B in his senior year.

Priest lists Harold Vogelsang as one of his three mentors. Vogelsang had served as an infantryman in World War I and had been active in youth work for many years. Vogelsang coached the young Priest not only on the baseball field but also in life. He encouraged him and assisted him in setting and attaining goals. Banks were not a secure place in the early thirties, so Vogelsang kept Priest's earnings in the safe at the police station. Protecting Priest's money from the unpredictability of the depression was just one more way Vogelsang helped Priest to secure his future. Giving Priest the opportunity to hone his pitching skills would open many doors.

After graduating from high school at age sixteen, the goal of being a history teacher still shone strong in Priest's vision. Teaching required a college education, and the taste of success on the baseball field turned his eyes toward the University of California at Berkeley, one of the premier universities in the United States, and where one of the best college baseball coaches, Clint Eans, worked. There were no scholarships, but that was not the first hurdle. Due to Priest's lack-luster sophomore year in high school, he was half a credit short and was not accepted at Berkeley.

It was then that Priest was introduced to the value of junior colleges. The junior college concept, uniquely American, was relatively new with the first public junior college opening in Joliet, Illinois in 1901. Twenty years later, Modesto Junior College opened in California. By 1934, it was one of thirty-eight junior colleges in California. Priest's half a credit deficit did not hinder his enrollment in Modesto Junior College, which allowed him to make up the high school credit, and to establish himself as academically solid. That spring, he was accepted at Berkeley as a second semester freshman and played on the freshman baseball team.

Priest quickly moved to the varsity team where he distinguished himself by being voted number one all-conference pitcher two of the three years he played. Additionally, he won the Golden Bear Blanket Award for lettering in baseball three years. His peers honored him by electing him as president of California's Big C (Letterman) Society and appointing him to the University's Athletic Council.

This was the middle of the Great Depression which saw everyone scrapping to pay bills and keep food on the table. Since Berkeley did not offer baseball scholarships, it was necessary for Priest to work while attending college. He worked during the summers and through the winter holiday breaks. That first summer, he earned $16.80 a week for a forty-eight hour week as a day laborer in a warehouse owned by Western States Grocery. While attending classes, he cleaned pots for an agricultural researcher, a job he obtained through the National Youth Administration. The pay was thirty-five cents an hour for fifty hours of work per month. To stretch his earnings, he surreptitiously ate some of the tomatoes, which were being grown for research. In addition, the job included five cents per hour transportation compensation which he saved by walking to and from the lab.

His sophomore year, Priest became the campus representative for a jewelry company that made fraternity and sorority jewelry. At seventeen, he was selling jewelry, cleaning pots, taking seventeen credit hours in college, and playing baseball. With all of this demand on his time, he still maintained a 3.0 grade point average.

Between his sophomore and junior years, he worked for the Calaveras Cement Plant. The pay was sixty cents an hour for twelve-hour days. The upside to that job was that he also earned money playing baseball for the Mother Lode League in the Angels Camp in the "jumping frog" county.

The following summer between his junior and senior years, Priest pitched in the California State League. They played each Sunday. He was paid $15 if they lost and $20 if they won. They won ten straight games. During the week, he worked as a gas and electric meter reader for $42.50 a week, one of his most lucrative jobs. The Pacific Gas and Electric Company gave each meter reader a book of addresses and no timeline to complete reading and recording the information from the houses and buildings listed for that day. Priest began at eight in the morning and typically finished in two and a half hours. In addition to offering good pay, this job also was one of the most interesting of all his jobs. Part of his territory was the rather large red light district in Stockton. Although he stood at the door shouting repeatedly, "meter reader," he often was mistaken for a customer. When a young woman would offer her services, Priest would explain the reason for his being there. Sometimes it was necessary to explain to several different ladies of the evening. Frequently a conversation would ensue and the topics were varied and always engaging.

The summer after graduation from Berkeley in 1938, the college baseball team barnstormed the country with a series of games beginning with Denver and ending with Dartmouth. The most delectable wins for Priest were over Harvard and Yale, both occurring in the same week. They were truly the boys of summer.

With autumn came a need to return to academics. After completing his bachelor's degree with his long-desired major in history and a minor in Spanish, Priest still needed graduate work to gain teaching credentials. But while working toward that end, his baseball talent loomed in the path of his original career goal.

Priest had an impressive combined record from the baseball team at the University of California, Berkeley, and the summer teams. He had pitched his college team to an intercollegiate championship with ten wins and two losses. He had a dramatic strikeout record of as many as sixteen in one game, and averaging twelve to fourteen in games where he started. He also had frequently saved the game as the relief pitcher. His pitching record was notable, and drew the attention of the scouts for the Boston Red Sox, the Chicago White Sox, and the Philadelphia Athletics. Priest chose to sign with the Philadelphia A's of the American League, the very team he had watched play just six years before. That, however, was not the deciding factor. Influencing his decision was an outfielder for the A's, Sam Chapman, who had been a teammate at Berkeley. Under the headline, "Bill Priest Knows What He's Doing," Lester Grant, a columnist for the *Stockton Record* newspaper, wrote on June 17, 1938, "Bill is a smart guy—he doesn't want to pitch against Chapman." In the few weeks Chapman had been with Philadelphia, he had hit nine homeruns. Grant added, "Priest probably will be a happy addition to the Philadelphia pitching fraternity, which is undoubtedly one of the weakest chucking corps in the major leagues."[1]

Philadelphia signed him for $450 a month, a salary above some with better records and with more experience. As today, the acquisition of a new player was done in hopes of improving the team's performance. The signing of Bill Priest to the Philadelphia team made the national papers and large headlines in Priest's hometowns of French Camp and Stockton. In an article from the Associated Press that ran in the *San Francisco Examiner*, Connie Mack was quoted as saying Priest was a good prospect and that he had not lost any games the last season in college ball. The editor added a note, "Oh, yes, Connie, Priest has been beaten, but we'll put in with you. He is good."[2]

Both of Priest's parents expressed faith in their son's abilities but neither gushed with excitement over his becoming a professional athlete. His mother praised his character and seemed to defend his choice from possible criticism of seeking stardom. Clarice Priest was quoted, "He is a fine boy, without a single bad habit and I just know he will make good. This is something his father and I are proud of. Bill has always been a home boy, and this will not change him at all. He is very serious and takes baseball very serious and has taken baseball as his life's work, so why shouldn't he be just as ambitious to become a great pitcher as others are to become great lawyers and writers?"[3]

Indeed, Priest was not of the nature to become enamored with his own accomplishments as would be reflected throughout the many successes of his life. He also proved to be a "home boy." Shortly after taking up residence with his new team, he wrote his parents that he was "wishful for home."[4]

A reporter for the *Stockton Record* caught Priest's father working on the ranch in French Camp, seven miles south of Stockton. Resting on his hoe, he gave an interview and seemed to play down the accomplishment of his son, which was his way, by responding, "The kid's all right. He takes right after his daddy, except that I was a catcher. He'll go right along."[5]

Twenty-four years earlier, when Jesse Priest played professional baseball in the Three-I league, he had been rated as one of the best semi-pro receivers in northern California. The interview noted that Jesse had been an enthusiastic supporter at most of his son's American Legion and college games.

Several of the local papers credited Harold Vogelsang, coach of the American Legion team, with grooming Priest for the majors. A quote from Vogelsang noted Priest was a natural, "He took to it like a duck to water. He learned fast. Besides, he could hit."[6]

For all the press, all the expectations, and all the praise of those who knew him, the glory days of junior league and college baseball were not duplicated on the professional fields of America's game. The following year, Priest was moved to the minor leagues. He describes his baseball career as "starting at the top and working my way down."[7] Neither did his performance in the Pacific Coast League equal his college success. Priest, who is never hesitant to site his weaknesses, tells it through the words of a Philadelphia fan, "I always laugh with a sting in it; a guy told me one time, 'Bill, you were a great college pitcher, but you forgot to bring your college hitters to hit against you.'"[8]

Although his professional baseball career was short-lived and according to Priest, the one thing at which he "was so immensely unsuccessful,"[9] it gave him leverage and brought him recognition throughout his career in higher education. People are always fascinated by anyone's brush with fame.

With professional baseball now just a line on Priest's resume, his career moved from one American invention to another, the junior college. In 1940, Priest accepted a position of coach and physical education teacher at Modesto Junior College where he had begun his own pursuit of a college degree seven years before. Only three additional junior colleges had opened in California since he first enrolled at Modesto. That was reflective of the junior college movement in the United States, steady but very slow. Even then, Priest had a sense that the junior college was the wave of the future.

CHAPTER TWO

The War Years

While a junior in college, Priest had been invited, along with most of the community, to the wedding of a rather prominent couple. He attended, and at the reception, he saw her again—the beautiful girl who used to ride horse back by his house, Marietta Shaw. The difference in grade-level had separated them in high school, but now he was close to being a college graduate, and she was an elementary teacher in French Camp. The chasm had closed, and she seemed approachable. The conversation was engaging and the attraction was mutual. They stepped outside the flurry of celebration and spent the remainder of the evening talking. Bill and Marietta stayed so late getting to know each other that Priest's ride left and he had to hitch-hike home.

Priest discovered that although he and Marietta had been separated by two grades in high school, there was in reality four years difference in age since he had skipped a grade, but years were irrelevant because the common interests and intellectual compatibility were so strong. They dated through his college graduation and his stint in professional baseball. As the relationship reached the point of commitment, he was teaching at Modesto Junior College and she, a music major, was teaching in elementary school. The local school board where she taught did not allow its female teachers to be married, so on March 8, 1941, Bill and Marietta eloped to Minden, Nevada. It was a small private ceremony held in the living room of a friend. The nuptials were presided over by a Lutheran minister. Marietta was Catholic and Priest believed in a supreme being but without affiliation to a particular denomination. The religion of the event was not as important to them as the legality of the lifetime vow they were making to each other.

Their jobs were sixty miles apart, and Marietta would be fired if the school board knew of her marriage, so they kept it a secret. Each Wednesday night, they would meet at a midpoint to have dinner and talk. The secret was kept until Marietta was offered a contract for the following year. She did not intend to continue teaching there, but she could not afford to have a firing on her record if she ever intended to teach again.

Life directions were a bit uncertain for the newlyweds. There was a war raging overseas and Priest felt that the United States could not continue its laissez-faire attitude much longer. He not only believed the U. S. involvement in the war was inevitable, but also that it was imminent. He was aware that he was of prime age to be drafted and felt that the likelihood of his returning from the war alive was slim. He decided that he should live as though he were going to be killed in a couple of years.

This abandonment of all that seemed rational and well planned might have frightened most young brides back to the safety of their mother's home, but Marietta shared Priest's spirit for adventure and love of the outdoors. They rented a cabin near a river just outside Stockton. She helped with the income by substitute teaching and he once again turned to his baseball skills for income. Priest pitched in the California State League on Sundays. He rested on Mondays; went trout fishing Tuesday through Friday, and rested on Saturday in preparation for Sunday's game. It was a Tom Sawyer summer.

Priest's prognosis proved right. By October 1, 1941, he was recruited and commissioned an Ensign in the Navy. He was assigned to Naval Intelligence and given two weeks of training in San Francisco in early November and returned home with open orders that simply directed, "If war begins, report here."[1]

Continuing to live life as if in his last weeks, he played out his love of sports in every day's activities. He was quail hunting in Sonoma, California on December 7, 1941. He was bringing in his kill for the day, one bird, when he ran into his father-in-law, who was the poultry man at Sonoma State Home. He told Priest about the bombing of Pearl Harbor. America was in the war. Priest reported to the office in San Francisco by seven p.m. that night. He was told to go home, get his things, and report back at eight a.m. the next morning. Priest arrived at his house in Mountain View at eleven p.m. where he had only a brief time to change from freelance sportsman to dedicated naval officer and to bid farewell to his wife of nine months, not knowing if they would ever see each other again.

Always punctual, he was back in San Francisco the following morning at eight a.m. His assignment was as officer in charge of Mackay radio operations. The duty station had two officers and nine men. Initially the work shifts covered seven days a week. A day off was assigned to each man, Priest's was Saturday. With the schedule being staggered eight-hour shifts, Priest ended up with fifty-six consecutive hours off-duty. Never one to be content with only one task, with approval from his superior officer, Priest enrolled in classes at Berkeley. This required loss of sleep, but it was for a limited time and the outcome would be worth it. His goal was to earn a Secondary Administrator Certificate. In his bachelor's degree he had majored in history and minored in Spanish. As he began his course work leading to a master's degree, he switched from letters and science to education.

After eight months, Priest was transferred to an instructor job in the Navy's Pre-Flight Program. Naval aviators were doing so well against the Japanese, Priest was soon reassigned again to Intelligence. Word came that he was being shipped to the Philippines; therefore, he did not enroll for a third semester at Berkeley. In a goodbye session, the head of the romance languages department encouraged Priest to pursue a doctorate. His plan for Priest was logical and efficient. In the Philippines, there would be a great opportunity to gather research on the war's impact on the educational system there. The Philippine education system was not a heavily researched topic, but one of interest to academia. Priest wanted to earn a master's degree first and was advised that the master's thesis could be the first chapter of a doctoral dissertation. In a truthful jest he was told that at the time of the defense of his dissertation, who but Priest would know more about such a distant and discrete subject? This should allow him to face the questioning by his committee and other university professors with confidence. The plan sounded strategic and quite doable, and Priest began the early steps in his pursuit of a doctorate.

During his stateside duty, Priest became friends with a man whose name he lists when asked who have been his heroes and mentors. Lt. Commander Curtis Peck was Priest's commanding officer for two years in Naval Intelligence. Peck did not have a formal education, but had an aptitude for understanding technology and had learned a great deal during a hitch as an enlisted radio man in World War I. In civilian life, he was the head engineer of RCA. Peck was proof that a liberal arts bachelor's degree was not the only route to a successful career, nor did the lack of a four-year degree indicate a lack of intelligence. He and Priest engaged in long philosophical discussions. The topics had no boundaries and covered everything from military personnel management to daily living in civilian life. Ensign Priest felt he was the recipient of valuable information and much wisdom from the Lt. Commander. Peck subsequently gave Priest a letter of entry to take to RCA in New York City and learn about the development of television in its infancy. At that time television was little more than a potential, but people in the field were forecasting long range and knew color broadcasts were just a few years away. Perhaps this early glimpse of things to come planted the seed for Priest's early exploration into televised instruction.

Most of Priest's overseas duty in the war was spent in the Philippines and Japan. While given assignments that kept him off the front lines, Priest, however, was not spared the visual horrors of war. His duties took him into areas where the population center had been wrested from the Japanese. His task involved ferreting out the location of guerrillas and assessing the damage to communication systems. This included being part of the advanced intelligence party that entered Hiroshima in 1945, shortly after the atomic bombing.

His first tour of overseas duty was in the Philippines. This was a mix of military duty, the hideous sights of war, and personal good fortune. The positive aspect was the incredible access he had to the educational leaders and their willingness to provide information. He took canned turkey to several Filipino leaders who had been incarcerated in a Catholic Church by the Japanese. The prisoners were Filipinos that the Japanese had held in high regard and had not thought of as threatening. This group of national leaders who had been liberated by the Americans included the senior educational officer of the Philippines, Santa Tomas. A Harvard graduate, Tomas was an internationally famous ethnologist. With his permission, Priest was given the freedom to interview people, ship files and materials back to Priest's address in the United States, and to disseminate a survey. Anyone who has done research is very pleased with a fifty percent return on a survey. Priest received a 106 percent return. Filipino educators who heard about the survey asked for copies in order to be able to participate, thus expanding the return. These surveys were sent to Tomas' office; from there he mailed them to Priest, after he returned to the states. Priest was overwhelmed and humbled by the desire of these people to assist American research of their educational system. Perhaps there was a hope it would bring improvements for them from the wealthy nation that now occupied their impoverished country.

The interviews and surveys took many weeks. A cliché often attributed to the military is "hurry up and wait." So it was for Priest. He had been given what was described as a hazardous assignment, but it was not known exactly when he would be deployed to carry out the plan. His superiors told him to just wait. He waited twenty-five days checking in each day only to be told it was not yet time.

He used that waiting time to interview and collect data for his thesis. After twenty-five days, he was told the plan had been changed and the Americans were no longer involved in that operation. His new assignment would be to go to Zambawango to hire and train a team of Filipinos in the censorship of communications. Again they were uncertain as to when he would leave. Again he waited. For another fifteen days, he was able to collect data for his research.

Even in the routine of daily life was the ever-present reminder of the terrible world trauma that had brought him there. He once saw a man walking down the beach carrying another man's head by the hair. The man told Priest he was taking it to the authorities to collect the bounty "on the man's head." The American English idiom of using the part to represent the whole had been taken literally in translation. After the fighting had ended, the devastation continued. Priest witnessed a group of Filipino fisherman who had found an unexploded torpedo and were gathering the powder from it to use in killing fish. These innocent fishermen knew little about explosives. While they were working on it, the torpedo exploded leaving no identifiable body parts. The events were gruesome and innumerable, forever etching in his memory sites and emotions difficult to discuss.

The experience in Japan was worse. Priest was part of the advance party to Hiroshima after the atomic bomb had been dropped on August 6, 1945. The members of this select team were the first Americans to enter the city as soon as the radio activity indicated it was safe. He recalled traveling down a road lined on each side with Japanese soldiers, their backs to the road. They were looking outward, protecting the Americans, who were their captors. The Emperor had issued an order and the Japanese were highly disciplined. Americans were no longer the enemy, but the honored victors. During the routine survey of the area, Priest saw people with indescribable injuries. He was struck with sorrow, apprehension, and empathy knowing that just days before, his countrymen used the most formidable weapon on earth on their city and within five minutes annihilated one-hundred-and-thirty-thousand people and destroyed ninety percent of the city. At the same time, Priest was filled with pride in being an American and knowing that by his country's action, many more lives had been saved. In President Harry Truman's radio address to the American public just sixteen hours after the bombing of Hiroshima, he explained, "The Japanese began the war from the air at Pearl Harbor. They have been repaid manyfold. . . . It was to spare the Japanese people from utter destruction that the ultimatum of July 26 was issued at Potsdam. Their leaders promptly rejected that ultimatum."[2]

As Priest went about his duties in Hiroshima, each person he saw or with whom he spoke was injured, had lost a loved one, or was close to someone who was critically wounded. He saw a man who had been looking out a window from miles away at the time of the bomb and the window shattered in his face. Like most who have served their country during a war, Priest was profoundly affected by the experience. It seemed to him that with all of the intelligence and problem solving mechanisms available to mankind, there should be a less violent means for resolving philosophical differences. He also was deeply disturbed by the poverty of the Orient, Philippines, and Manila. The suffering of these people in their daily struggles to live washed against the backdrop of the horrors of war, death, and destruction, underscored for Priest that one must do what is important each day. Life is temporary and fleeting, and to make a difference for your fellowman, later is not a time option.

The end of the war came and Priest mustered out of the Navy on February 16, 1945, but continued in the U.S. Naval Reserve. With his combined full-time and part-time duty, he retired as a captain with twenty years of service. Like baseball, his military career, most specifically his immediate arrival in Hiroshima after the atomic bomb, gave him a certain notoriety throughout his higher education career. It was the end of the war and the return of the G.I.s to the United States that caused the surge of the junior college, that wave of the future Priest had visualized in the mid-1930s.

CHAPTER THREE

The Wave Swells

After returning stateside and to civilian life, Priest continued his studies full-time for his master's degree at the University of California Berkeley. He completed it in May, 1946. Utilizing some of those graduate courses toward the doctorate and his master's thesis, "Administration of Philippine Education Under the Commonwealth Government," as the first chapter of his dissertation, "Philippine Education in Transition," he earned his Ed. D. from Berkeley a year later, in May of 1947.

Priest's war assignment had assisted in his collection of data and had given him the rare opportunity to research a subject for which no other North American academician would have the same knowledge base as he. Finding the time to write had not been a challenge. Priest had acquired a job teaching algebra and basic math at Mountain View, a high school in the Bay Area of northern California. The classes took little preparation for him and allowed him to work on his dissertation from three p.m. to eleven p.m. each weekday. Gaining approval for his dissertation to move to the next step of defense with the University's committee was unusually simple. He took the document to his major professor who held it

in his hand, looked Priest in the eye and asked, "Is it a good dissertation?" Priest, sensing this was not a time for humility, replied,
"It's a hell of a good dissertation." With a nod, the professor returned the dissertation to Priest and said simply, "It's approved."
At the defense, however, an assistant professor of history tried to
demonstrate his knowledge and perhaps his worthiness of a full
professor's position by challenging Priest's data, but a senior professor took the assistant professor to task. The defense ended with
handshakes for the new member into the community of scholars,
Dr. Bill Jason Priest.

No dissertation reaches its final placement on the shelves of the
graduate library without its author suffering some. After his dissertation had been defended, signed by the appropriate professors
and deans, and delivered to the office of the dean of the College
of Education, Priest was informed that he needed to write a five-
hundred word abstract. He did so promptly and delivered it to the
office of the dean. Soon afterwards on a spring morning while he
was teaching math, Priest was called out of class to take a telephone
call from the dean of the graduate division. Over the telephone, a
secretary told Priest that he could not graduate because his abstract was over five-hundred words. With all the emotions of panic,
disappointment, anger, and frustration raging at once, Priest left
his job with a copy of the abstract and drove the sixty miles to Berkeley. When he arrived, the secretary was sitting at her desk. With
the questioned abstract in hand, Priest told her he had carefully
counted and recounted the words and each time found there to
be no more than five-hundred. With a sigh she said, "I could have
sworn it was over five-hundred words."[1]

Having been taken from his teaching assignment, run through
an emotional wringer, and caused to drive an hour-and-a-half, based
on a secretary's miscalculation, Priest felt this must be dealt with.
He asked to see the dean. He recounted the events, to which the
dean responded with a comforting smile and the affirmation of an
old sage, "Well, it's O.K. now." It was not the response Priest felt
was appropriate, but certainly being allowed to graduate on schedule was the more important outcome.

Following graduation, Priest spent the next year as the Educational Advisor to the Navy Retraining Command. This quasi-school was part of the Navy's penal system. Prisoners under General Court Martial who were deemed to be good prospects for rehabilitation were trained and made ready for a return to society.

In the fall of 1948, Priest assumed his first junior college administrative role in Costa Mesa, California, at Orange Coast College, which was opening on a remodeled Air Force base. California was the bellwether state in the two-year college movement and by 1948 boasted sixty-four such institutions of higher learning. Junior colleges were being established throughout the United States during the first half of the twentieth century, but the growth and acceptance was slow until World War II, when there was a wave of support for the returning soldiers. The colleges were struggling to take virtually all students regardless of preparation, and this open-door philosophy of admission, for which community colleges are now renowned, enticed a wide range of talent and abilities. The universities were not willing to enroll the under-prepared, and it was the fast changing junior college that was best equipped to respond to this need. In 1947, the United States President's Commission on Higher Education published a report calling for an increase in the number of junior colleges and for the diversification of their offerings. This began the evolution of the junior college into the community college. The country needed a better trained work force for the growing industries, and greater access to higher education would encourage social equality. John Aubrey Douglas in his book, *The California Idea and American Higher Education*, said that the junior college was seemingly two institutions in one: a college serving as a stepping stone to the university, and a technical school that trained the labor force for emerging industries. This schizophrenia still characterizes the modern day community college.[2] It is often the cause of internal conflicts within a single college. Priest was to fight that battle later in his career.

Serving as the dean and then later the assistant superintendent of Orange Coast College District, Priest worked for another of his "heroes" and mentors, Basil Peterson. Peterson had been a basketball player, a Phi Beta Kappa, and a highly sought after godfather, having many godchildren. He was a professional and personal friend to Priest. Peterson gave Priest opportunities to do projects beyond the scope of his job as learning experiences. Peterson knew the value of being a generalist in higher education especially in leadership roles, where a breadth of understanding is necessary to make well grounded decisions. But once again, the religious example for Priest was that of a fundamentalist. Although Peterson was Mormon rather than First Christian, Priest saw in him a dedicated church participant like his grandfather. Peterson was straight-laced and inflexible, but he was intelligent and a superb educator and leader.

While at Orange Coast, Priest helped to precipitate one of the most significant changes in higher education, the movement of nurses' training from the hospitals to colleges. S. H. Fondiller wrote, in a book published in 1983 by the National League of Nursing, that the movement of nursing education from privately controlled hospitals to the general education system and the development of the associate degree in nursing (ADN) was one of the most important developments in the history of education in this country. Priest was a part of that movement.[3]

Again it was World War II that targeted the need for significant changes in higher education. It made the nation acutely aware of the shortage of nurses. Twenty-three percent of the hospitals in the United States were forced to close beds, wards and/or operating rooms. By 1951, the idea of total collegiate nursing education was growing. As early as 1949, the National League of Nursing Education (NLNE) was meeting with the American Association of Junior Colleges (AAJC, now American Association of Community Colleges or AACC) to discuss a nursing technician program. A large percentage of physicians and hospital administrators opposed nurses taking control of planning the type of education appropriate for their profession. They called it self-serving. At that time, about eighty diploma programs were offered in association with hospitals, but there were no separate college programs. At the national level, Edmund J. Gleazer, executive director of the AAJC, was a primary participant in meetings with the NLNE. Ed Gleazer was involved at the national level through Kellogg Foundation Funding. Priest was working primarily at the state level in California which was spearheading the new concept, and later he served on national committees related to nursing.

In 1953, Priest was assistant superintendent of Orange Coast and remembered the uphill battle with the medical profession, "They thought we were trying to kill people and contaminate hospitals with heavy-handed nurses who didn't know what they were doing. It almost seemed they'd sooner see people die from a shortage of BSN's [Bachelor of Science in nursing] than to turn loose what they considered to be this horde of unwashed." The meetings seemed endless with little progress being made due to the medical professionals "with their holier-than-thou" attitudes. Priest recalled, "You could present statistics; here's the staffing, here's the supply that the current training for nursing is providing. Look at this gap. How are you going to do it? Are you going to call people in off the street? That's what you're doing now. And they'd reply, 'Yes, but they are under the guidance of a BSN.' We'd point out that there wouldn't be a BSN within shouting distance, and they'd promise to close that gap if we wouldn't contaminate the profession. Well it got contaminated and now [the associate degree] is accepted and produces the majority of bedside registered nurses in the nation."[4]

At Orange Coast, Priest offered one of the first pilot nursing programs in the country. It was successful and the growth in the associate degree in nursing programs was steady through the 1950s. There was an explosion in the 1960s and by 1964, 130 associate degree nursing programs were being offered and represented eleven percent of all registered nursing programs. In 1965, the National League for Nursing Education created a separate associate degree program component and called for separate accreditation. Again, Priest was ready at the helm and selected the first college of the Dallas Junior College District, El Centro, to be the first two-year college in Texas to offer an ADN program. That program produces over two-hundred graduates each year with an average of ninety-nine percent passing the National Nursing Boards.[5]

While a large percentage of his time was spent on curriculum development and academic related issues, Priest was keenly aware that being an effective leader and educator took more than offering relevant courses. In the fall of 1954, he enrolled in post-doctoral study in community relations at Columbia University. This formal study helped to hone Priest's natural marketing acumen. He was far ahead of his time in this area. Marketing and public relations were not acceptable concepts in higher education for most of its history. While Priest used his public relation skills in all of the colleges where he worked, it was in Dallas where he helped to make marketing a palatable word for educators. Wide acceptance has been slow and recent.

A key concept of good marketing is listening to your customers. Marketing was a very uncomfortable word for educators who inferred a limited connotation as "selling." The members of the community are a college's customers because they "buy" the courses the college offers. Not all are seeking advanced degrees or even vocational degrees. Many simply want information, knowledge, and training in a particular area. Priest was aware of the value of non credit courses and it was at Orange Coast he realized the real value of listening to the people served by that college. A woman came to Priest's office asking for a course in goat husbandry. Priest listened, albeit with great skepticism. Believing in fact-based decision making, the college had a policy that it would offer any non credit course petitioned for with a minimum of fifteen signatures. He explained the policy to the woman who returned in a few days with a petition with more than the required fifteen signatures. The following semester he offered the course and sixty people enrolled. He then discovered they were the only college offering the course within a fifty-mile radius. Intermediate and advanced goat husbandry courses were added to the schedule of classes and met with equal success. Again utilizing excellent marketing, Priest reminded the reporters who showed interest in the phenomenal success of the goat husbandry courses that a university would have thrown the woman out and left all of those tax paying citizens without the courses they needed.

Priest's reputation as an innovative, risk-taking but budgetarily sound leader in higher education was growing among his colleagues. His responsiveness to the constituents served by his college district, his community involvement, and his being a devoted family man who had been married for eighteen years with an eleven year old son, earned him the admiration of the community as well. In 1959, he was named "Man of the Year" in Fair Oaks, California. Every accolade that came his way was accepted with a dismissal as good fortune and good timing. His focus remained on quality instruction and the development of relevant courses whether purely academic, vocational, or not for college credit.

Non credit classes and credit classes often clashed in the battle for space with the non credit classes being given last choice. At Orange Coast College, the only space available for a popular millinery class was a biology lab. Through a series of events during a biology class, a tarantula escaped and was not found that day. The millinery instructor was left a note, "tarantula loose in classroom." Fortunately the fierce looking little creature never made itself known in the totally female class. While a rather humorous demonstration of the space issues in junior colleges, the real battle, the so called schizophrenia of junior colleges, is the battle of pure academics versus vocational courses, even when they are both for credit.

Nowhere was that more of an issue than at American River College, which opened in Sacramento, California in 1955. Priest was hired as the Superintendent/President of the new college. He had the arduous task of not only beginning a new college, but also absorbing an existing college, Grant Technical College, into the new organizational structure. Grant Technical College had actually been the top two years of a kindergarten through fourteenth grade school in the local public school district. The faculty of the college levels, however, had tenure. That was the first hurdle. The new college being founded would not have tenure for the faculty. This was one of the first conflicts. The established faculty felt they should be grandfathered in the non-tenure for faculty policy. They sued and won. Now Priest was faced with a faculty in which some had tenure and some did not. Many of the former faculty of Grant Technical

College felt that none of the new rules should apply to them. This perpetual problem more than doubled the efforts of establishing a new college. There were continual lawsuits and the attorney was less than competent. He lost nine cases out of nine. Fortunately the Board of Trustees gave full support to Priest in the challenges he faced. In Priest's estimation, they were a quality board with a focus on the educational good for students.

Not one to become mired down in the negativity of disputes and disagreements, Priest remained focused on the mission of the college and the quality of courses and services being offered to students. Marketing the concept he believed in was also at the forefront of his goals. With a mix of humor, a bit of ego, and a marketing goal, Priest adopted the bow tie as his trademark. His reasoning was that it was different from what other men were wearing. He said that when he spoke at an event or met with community leaders, or was simply introduced to someone at a gathering, they might not remember his name, but they would always remember "that guy with the bow tie." His bow tie was as significant as the logo for American River College because he promoted the value of junior and community colleges wherever he went.

On the national level, during his tenure as the CEO of American River College, Priest was actively involved in growing the purpose and visibility of the American Association of Junior Colleges. The association was founded in 1920, but it was not far reaching or political. Initially the main focus was for these early educational pioneers to come together to define the junior college by creating standards for curriculum and determining the position of the junior college in relationship to other parts of the American education enterprise. The junior college had its roots in rural America, but the rapid expansion since World War II was taking the junior college movement into urban areas.

Among those college leaders was Edmund J. Gleazer, who later headed AAJC. At this time he was the president of Graceland College, a church-related junior college that had begun as a four-year institution. Graceland had consolidated its resources into a two-year institution on the advice of William Rainey Harper of the

University of Chicago, with assurances the university would take their graduates. With the involvement of Gleazer, Priest, and other junior college leaders of like mind, the AAJC broadened its purpose to educate the federal government to the value of this fast-growing aspect of higher education that was embraced by the American public. The Foundations that were beginning to offer grant opportunities in the areas of education seemed to overlook the junior colleges. It became a priority of the membership to send someone to Washington D.C. with the specific task of garnering more national visibility to the worth and potential of junior colleges. Priest was very supportive of a more aggressive role of AAJC and a presence in Washington. His support was critical because the California Junior College Association was big and powerful, but many of its members were skeptical about the need for a national association. Gleazer, who had served as president of the association, was selected to serve in the special task position to work with the AAJC head, Jesse P. Bogue in Washington. In 1958, Gleazer was elected executive director of AAJC to replace Bogue upon his retirement. Priest and Gleazer continued to work together as colleagues with a common goal. Gleazer said that Priest was well respected in the state of California and assisted him in arranging meetings with the junior college leadership in that state.[6]

Remaining in Sacramento, California, Priest was selected as superintendent of Los Rios Junior College District. The district was newly formed from two colleges, American River College, where he was serving as president, and Sacramento City College. This was not the melding of an established faculty with a new faculty, but the merger brought its own set of challenges. The new board consisted of members from each of the colleges. This created a four-to-three split vote on virtually everything, occasionally even the minutes from the last board meeting.

The second year as superintendent of Los Rios Junior College District, Priest was elected vice-president of AAJC. The following year he would be elected president of the association, an indication of historical protocol. The board might have been split in its support, but his colleagues across the country were unified in recognition of his accomplishments in the evolution of community colleges.

It was while at Los Rios that Priest pioneered another innovation in higher education, the telecourse. The husband of a former classmate of Priest was the president of the Public Broadcasting Services (PBS) station for the area. Television was still a relatively new medium and the PBS station had time to fill in its daytime programming schedule. The time was offered to the college. Realizing the potential of television to reach additional students who were not able to come to campus, Priest accepted the on-air time slot and offered a history course. It was purely experimental. Even in the early sixties, a high percentage of television programs were live. All local programming was live. The only production for the history course was a minimal classroom set in a bare studio with one camera. The live head-on shot format was fraught with problems that greatly cut into the quality, but the response from the public was good. Priest battled the State of California for reimbursement for those students who never came to campus. He could see the potential, but knew the format needed polishing. All of the possible problems that could exist for a single class on campus— the need for the instructor to be on time, well prepared, and contingencies in case the instructor was ill—existed for the televised class, with additional technical issues, and a wider impact on more students if something went wrong. On one occasion, the instructor arrived for the broadcast inebriated. The television station manager telephoned Priest and asked him what he should do about the situation. Priest replied that he could not remember the part of his graduate courses that explained how to handle the matter. The man's condition was not discernable to the viewing audience and the class was broadcast as usual. Priest kept the idea of televised education alive and mentally filed for future use, with refinements. He would have such an opportunity in Dallas.

Dallas was one of the first twenty major cities to establish a junior college. This boom in the junior college movement occurred in the mid-sixties. In 1965 alone, fifty-two new two-year colleges opened. This wrought a bit of a crisis in the need for qualified personnel to fill all of the new leadership positions. To address the issue, the American Association of Junior Colleges and the Kellogg Foundation initiated the development of junior and community college leadership graduate programs. AAJC and Kellogg brought into partnership ten of the larger universities in the country to offer doctoral programs. These programs were funded by grants from the Kellogg Foundation but each university developed its own curriculum and degree requirements. The University of Texas in Austin, under the direction of C. C. Colvert, was one of the ten. There were four higher education administrators selected by the Kellogg Foundation to monitor and evaluate the ten projects. Priest was one of the four and the only one from a two-year college district.

There was not only a need to provide educational preparation for college leaders, but also, a need to educate the many newly appointed/elected board of trustee members in the multifaceted aspects of the mission, organizational structure of junior and community colleges, and how to begin to plan. Based on that need, AAJC commissioned Priest to write an article on the selection of a college president. The article, titled simply "Selecting a College President," was published in the *American Association of Junior College Journal* in the April issue of 1965. It became the first link between Priest and the Board of Trustees of Dallas County Junior College District.

CHAPTER FOUR

The Dallas Story

Establishing the District
and Hiring the President

There were early attempts at establishing the junior college in the Dallas area, but those built in the late 1800s did not survive. The junior college movement did not reach fruition in Dallas until the mid-1960s when two-year colleges were being opened nationally on the average of one per week.[1] Efforts toward the establishment of a junior college for the Dallas area had been underway in one form or another for a decade. The delays hinged on two main issues: whether the college should serve just the city or the entire county, and whether it should be associated with a public school district or should be a separate entity.[2]

The first aborted attempt began in 1956 when the Dallas Independent School District (DISD) appointed a Junior College Committee, and commissioned C. C. Colvert from the University of Texas to conduct a feasibility study. That study would include an indication of the interest on the part of the Dallas citizenry in having a junior college. In July of 1958, DISD superintendent, W. T. White withdrew the plans. There was concern that the establishment of a desegregated city college would have implications for public grades of kindergarten through the twelfth.[3] The Dallas school district was not integrated until the late sixties. It was an issue some educational leaders were not ready to address in the late fifties.

Dallas was not without a college. Southern Methodist University opened in 1915, but it was not founded with the intent of providing education to residents of the greater Dallas area. Priest described it at that point in time as "a regional sectarian institution, characterized by substantial tuition fees and a selective admissions policy."[4] This left a vacuum in higher education in Dallas County. Dallas residents who had transportation or could not afford to stay in the dormitories had to rely on perimeter state colleges in Denton, Arlington, and Commerce, or travel even farther and be forced to live at that college. The closest junior colleges were Kilgore and Tyler, each ninety or more miles from Dallas.

In 1960, the Dallas County Board of School Trustees and County Superintendent L. A. Roberts, became interested in a junior college to serve all of Dallas County. Colvert's earlier study supported the need and receptivity of the residents for a county-wide college district.[5] The board appointed a committee to conduct a study on the need for a Dallas County junior college. In March of 1962, Roberts wrote to the educational chair of the Dallas Chamber of Commerce indicating that he felt public interest would be necessary to make the college system a reality and that the study, "should be generated as promptly as is feasible." As recorded in J. D. Williams' unpublished dissertation at the University of Texas in 1968, Roberts further stated the board's readiness "to cooperate with any conservative plan for the youth of junior college age in Dallas County."[6] This was a monumental statement in that it sparked the chain of events that resulted in the Dallas County Community College District. Roberts, however, was myopic in his view of the educational needs of Dallas County being limited to recent high school graduates. While the evolution of demographics has been slower for universities, junior colleges burgeoning in the post war years attracted and served a wide range of students of all ages. The same was true for Dallas.

While the study commissioned by the Dallas County Board of School Trustees was being conducted, both the Grand Prairie Independent School District and the Richardson Independent School District were planning for junior colleges in each of their cities. Richardson had actually taken legal steps toward the establishment of a junior college, but the move was defeated at the polls October 27, 1962. Richardson voters were fearful of footing the bill for a facility that would serve an entire county. They were also concerned that the six existing four-year institutions within a fifty mile radius of Richardson would entice their local high school graduates from attending the junior college and it would lack adequate enrollment.[7] The opening of Richland College just six years later would prove that to be an unwarranted fear.

In the spring of 1964, the still segregated Dallas Independent School District surveyed the parents of their students and found overwhelming support for a junior college.[8] Armed with this data, the DISD board chair, Robert Gilmore, announced intentions to move forward with the building of an integrated junior college that would offer a variety of educational courses, but once again the issue of a city college versus a county college surfaced. The DISD served residents of the city of Dallas only. Its tax base was also drawn from the city and did not allow for support of a college that would serve the entire county. This would exclude the numerous growing suburbs of the city of Dallas. Superintendent White was not ready to admit defeat.[9]

While the DISD controversy continued, the Dallas Chamber of Commerce was busy gathering twenty-two of the most successful and influential business people in Dallas as a steering committee to form a plan of action to establish a Dallas County junior college. The committee was headed by R. L. (Bob) Thornton, Jr., who later became the first chair of the board of the Dallas County Junior College District.[10]

With the Dallas Chamber of Commerce firmly behind them, the steering committee wasted no time in accomplishing its assigned task. The development of an outstanding junior college system was listed as goal number five in *The Goals for Dallas* formulated by a diverse committee under the watchful eye of Mayor Erik Jonsson.[11] In April of 1964, Thornton addressed the State Board of Education requesting ratification of the proposal for establishing a junior college in Dallas County. The momentum was in place and just one year and one month later, the voters of Dallas passed a 41.5 million dollar bond issue with a two-to-one margin.[12] That vote officially established the county-wide junior college system with a mandate from the people of Dallas County. In that same election on May 25, 1965, the voters also approved a property tax base for the junior college system of sixteen cents per one hundred dollars of appraised property value, and they elected seven unopposed board of trustee members.[13]

Although the voters of Dallas elected the founding Board of Trustees, because they ran unopposed on the ballot, they were actually hand-picked from the most dedicated and capable of the civic leaders of Dallas. Selection had been made by a subcommittee of the original steering committee. The subcommittee was headed by Juvenile Court Judge Lewis Russell, who guided them through a selection process from a list of seventy names provided by Thornton.[14] Those selected and then elected were Durwood Sutton, Carie Welch, Loncy Leake, Frank Altick, Margaret McDermott, Franklin Spafford, and Bob Thornton.

Each elected board member was a professional, a respected member of the community, and a civic leader. Thornton was the chairman of the board of the Mercantile Bank and the son of R. L. Thornton, Sr., known as "Mr. Dallas" for his leadership in developing the city. Spafford was an attorney and served as the lawyer for the Dallas Independent School District. McDermott, the only woman, was the wife of Eugene McDermott, the co-founder of Texas Instruments. McDermott was and still is one of Dallas's foremost patrons of the arts. Altick was a medical doctor who owned and operated a clinic in north Dallas. Leake was a lawyer in private practice in Mesquite. Welch was the Mayor Pro Tem of Dallas and an insurance agent living in Oak Cliff. Sutton was the president of Grand Prairie State Bank. Every sector of Dallas was represented by these seven citizens.

After the successful election on May 25, the avidity of each of the new board members to bring to fruition this keenly needed junior college created a synergy of immediacy for a single purpose. They held their first meeting six days later on May 31, 1965. An outline of duties was distributed and officers were elected. Thornton was elected president; McDermott, vice-president; and Spafford, secretary.[15] They were well aware of the expansive task before them, but they were equally aware of the idealistic circumstances underlying that task. They were the prosopopoeia of the words of Margaret Mead, "Never doubt that a small group of thoughtful citizens can change the world; indeed, it is the only thing that can."[16] This board was positioned to bring monumental changes to the educational opportunities for the citizens of Dallas County, who then would affect far-reaching changes.

In an interview in July 1994, Margaret McDermott recounted, "There we were; seven people with the money we needed and none of us truly expert in designing a college. We used consultants; but from the very first, we wanted the very best."[17] As a self-acknowledgment of their own lack of experience in developing an institution of higher education, the board decided not to set any policies or write any by-laws until after consulting with experts in the field and after the hiring of a president. They did not want a new president shackled to prescribed tools of management. In that first meeting, Thornton had admonished the group that as trustees, every act and thought must be in the best interest of the junior college. The board began its search for guidance.[18]

An obvious source of excellent advice was the American Association of Junior Colleges. Ed Gleazer was the executive president at the time. In November of 2002 he detailed that first meeting with Thornton. It was a late spring day when Thornton arrived at the AAJC Washington D.C. office without an appointment. The secretary informed Gleazer that a Mr. Bob Thornton from Dallas was in the office and would like to see him. Thornton entered the office with robust confidence and in his straight forward style said, "The voters in Dallas County have voted to authorize a junior college district, elected a board of seven trustees, and authorized a tax levy and power to issue bonds. We will have the best damn junior college in the country and we need a president to do the job for us. Can you help us?" Gleazer was taken aback for a moment. Then he noticed the recently published issue of the *AAJC Journal* sitting on the corner of his desk. He recommended that Thornton read the featured article "Selecting a College President" by Bill Priest. He assured him the article would be helpful and then added that Thornton might want to take a look at the author.[19]

Thornton and the other board members not only read the article, but also followed the prescription it gave for "making the most important decision the board will ever make . . . for the institution's future will reflect the wisdom of the choice."[20] The article went on to warn, "With the rapid growth of the junior college movement, the importance of securing the best available talent for the key position of chief administrator cannot be overemphasized."[21] This fit with the goal of the Dallas board to hire the finest college administrator in the country.

Priest's article called for identifying long-range goals for the institution through the process of developing pertinent questions related to what the board was looking for in a president. The article cited the following examples:

1. What are the major objectives of the college?
2. Are there peculiar local factors which will affect the type of person being sought?
3. Is the board seeking a man who will make a career as a chief administrator of the college, or do they want a special job done (i.e. a building program) by a person who has great ability in this particular field, but who may not be a generalist?
4. What role does the board expect the president to play in the administration of the college? Is the objective to obtain a president who will supply strong educational leadership to the college, including recommendations for future plans, or is it to employ a person to implement plans which have already crystallized?[22]

The questions were insightful and somewhat prophetic in that the profile that emerged as the new board members fleshed out answers was a profile well-fitted to the knowledge and experience of Priest.

The article also suggested developing formal criteria for the initial screening of candidates. The four general areas given were: academic training and credentials, experience, personal characteristics, and educational philosophy. Also, the article outlined a good method for developing a credible list of potential candidates. By drawing from junior college specialists from universities, and leaders from state and national junior college associations, a screening committee could be established whose members were well acquainted with top junior college professionals. The committee could recommend candidates to be interviewed for the position of president.[23]

Following the hiring model set forth in Priest's article, the board sought the advice of C. C. Colvert of the University of Texas Department of Higher Education, and the one who had conducted the original feasibility study for a junior college in Dallas. They once again drew on the expertise of Gleazer. They asked for a list of about twenty outstanding junior college leaders from whom they could obtain criteria information and recommendations on possible candidates for the job. Both men gave similar lists of names. The Dallas board then invited this select group to Dallas for a few days of consulting with offers to pay their expenses and a small stipend. Nearly all indicated that they were happy to serve as a consultant, but they were not interested in the job. By the third or fourth interview, the value of the process became obvious. The board members began to assess the philosophies and backgrounds of the consultants as well as the men they were recommending. The list of final candidates included some of the consultants.[24]

Priest had been suggested by both Gleazer and Colvert to serve as a consultant. In talking with Priest about the establishment of criteria and the selection of a viable candidate, one of the board members asked Priest what he thought would be an appropriate salary for this new position. He indicated it would take thirty-five thousand dollars to bring someone to Dallas to take on this exciting challenge. In 1965, that sum rivaled the salary of the governor of Texas. This answer proved to be an example of Priest's unfaltering honesty, because some weeks later when he was offered the job and asked to name the amount it would take to lure him to Texas, Priest simply replied, "I told you when I was here before that I thought it would take thirty-five thousand dollars and I still think that would be a fair deal." The board agreed.[25]

On August, 4, 1965, less than three months after the bond election, Priest was offered a five-year contract at thirty-five thousand dollars a year, making him the highest paid top official of any state institution in Texas, including the governor.[26] Priest came to the job under the best conditions. He had been selected unanimously by the seven board members. There was adequate financing. He was to build a college from scratch with no mergers or pre-existing disharmony among staff. He could select his own staff. He could recommend policy to the board. There was an existing support from a friendly press. It was an ideal combination of circumstances.

The support of the news media was affirmed immediately. Following the press release that indicated the thirty-five thousand dollars annual salary for Priest making him one of the highest paid junior college executives in the nation, the *Dallas Morning News* ran an article, "Poised for Success," that never criticized the board for its commitment of taxpayer money at such a level. [27] It fully complimented their choice stating, "Because success breeds success, the newly elected Board of Trustees succeeded in obtaining the services of Dr. Bill J. Priest, one of the top men in his field, who this year is first vice president of the National Association of Junior Colleges."[28]

There was prevailing acceptance that the salary indicated a willingness on the part of the board to hire the very best in its quest to build a paramount community college system. Thornton underscored this idea when he publicly said, "The salary and the man are commensurate with the institution of highest excellence being planned for Dallas County."[29] There was no evidence that the news media or the citizens of Dallas ever disagreed with that philosophy. The article in the *Dallas Morning News* that ran the quote from Thornton justifying the top dollar salary, took no issue with the amount. Instead, the reporter introduced the new president to his readers as "a nationally recognized junior college authority" and "a superior administrator and educator deeply admired by those in the forefront of the community college movement."[30] The article stressed that Priest had been the Dallas County Junior College board's first and only choice for the job.

This unilateral backing by both the board and the local news media was contrary to the environment in which Priest had been working in Sacramento. The vote was consistently split for the Los Rios board members because each was loyal to one of the original two colleges that had been merged into one. Priest indicated that the only unanimous vote he ever received was the one releasing him from his contract to come to accept the Dallas job. He quipped, "My friends were happy for me and my enemies were glad to see me go."[31] The unanimous vote of the Dallas board for Priest was refreshing.

Priest was equally surprised and pleased to find the positive reporting of the local press. In California, the norm seemed to be for the news media to take an adversarial role with the administration of institutions of higher education. Even modest raises could create accusatory headlines. Priest remembered that his friend, the president of Yuba College in California, was given a raise from eighty-five-hundred-dollars to ten-thousand-dollars, and was greeted the following day with a front page photo and headline asking, "Is this man worth $10,000?" The newspaper article called for the ouster of the irresponsible board that made this decision. In sharp contrast, shortly after the announcement of Priest's being hired at an annual salary of fourteen-thousand-dollars above the president of the University of Texas, an editorial appeared in one of the major daily newspapers in Dallas extolling the integrity of the Dallas County Junior College Board for being willing to spend the money to bring in the very best leadership for the new junior college system. Priest said he sent a copy of the Dallas editorial to his friend in California with a note, "You're working in the wrong place. There seems to be a little difference in outlook." Priest kept copies of both the California front page article and the Dallas editorial beside each other for years, a reminder of his good lot.[32]

Priest did not take the solidarity of the board, the lucrative salary package, which also included a thirty-six-hundred-dollar annuity, and the overwhelming advocacy of the press and the community as a comfortable situation where one could feel secure. Instead, he viewed it as a seemingly insurmountable challenge of expectations of greatness. When he realized the unquestioning support was generated by the anticipation of the wonders to come and that he was the person expected to work that magic, he was humbled and intensely challenged. He described his feelings about the situation in a personal interview in 1994. "The thing that does to you, and I think this is obvious, is put you under incredible pressure. You want to perform miracles every hour on the hour if they put that kind of confidence in you. Your feeling is they deserve the best. We have got to deliver it some damn way. Whatever it is we have to figure it out because with this kind of support you ought to be able to be a paragon of virtue every minute. You can't fight off critics by saying, 'oh, to hell with them,' and you get righteously indignant. But the only room in a deal like this is you feel terribly inadequate. You think, 'I can't possibly do what is expected of me,' but you can try like hell."[33] Priest not only tried, he succeeded. His humble self-effacing assessment of the situation was sincere and part of what kept him perpetually in high gear to rise to meet those expectations, and, of course, his own indomitable drive to achieve the best in all endeavors.

When first hired, Priest was constantly hearing and reading about his being the obvious best for the job. Thornton was quoted in *Southwest Scene Magazine*, a Sunday supplement to the *Dallas Morning News*, "Priest stood out head and shoulders above anyone we interviewed and when the decision was made, the trustees were convinced they had the best junior college administrator in the country."[34] He was pelted by accolades which set a high bar for him. It also piqued his curiosity about what the true decisive factor had been for the board in selecting him.

The six-hour interview had been held at the Lancers Club on the top floor of the building. Priest had been described as looking like a cross between a prize fighter and Papa Bear, not presidential looking. On that occasion, he wore a checkered sport coat and his trademark bow tie. During the interview, one trustee had whispered to another, "Don't look at him; just listen to him."[35]

Priest described the interview as a love-fest in that there had been immediate rapport. There had not been a litany of grueling questions. Instead, it had been more like a convivial conversation. He knew there had to have been something deeper that drove the final decision.

One day over lunch, after Priest had spent a period of time in the DCJC job, he asked board member Franklin Spafford, an attorney by profession, what it was that had brought the committee to the conclusion that he was the best professional for the job, and what had caused them to offer the job so quickly. Priest told Spafford he was aware of the quality candidates from across the country who the committee had interviewed and therefore, was surprised by the short amount of time between his interview and their extending the job offer to him. Priest confessed that he had hoped Spafford's reply would give some insight into the answers he had given that day and that he might discover what had distinguished him from the others.

Spafford responded to the forthright questions with complete honesty. The interview had begun at six p.m., the cocktail hour, and so everyone had ordered drinks. Spafford reminded Priest that each of the twenty-two committee members ordered a fine wine or a mixed drink, some with special requirements. Priest ordered last. At the end of all those precise and sophisticated orders, he said, "If it's all right with you, I think I'll have a beer." Spafford explained that with that order they knew Priest was a man of the people and that he was honest and a risk taker. Spafford went on to say that some of the other candidates had ordered drinks with great specificity, sometimes to the point of giving a recipe for the drink with instructions for the bartender on how to mix it. The committee had agreed that extreme efforts to impress a level of sophistication was very telling and did not leave a positive impression. Priest was completely without pretensions and at ease with who he was.[36]

Although the answer was somewhat deflating to his ego, Priest indicated he loves to tell the story when he is presenting to high level professionals on the art of interviewing. A guileless drink order won him what he calls the best job of his career. While his genuineness set him apart in the interview, his steadfast honesty and integrity were only a few of the characteristics that earned him a place at the table.

The trustees held a press conference following the Dallas County Junior College board meeting where they formally approved the recommendation of the Committee of the Whole. At that conference, Priest gave a prepared response in which he delivered all the appropriate amenities, extolled the junior college as a concept, made a promise of educational service to the people of Dallas County, and proffered a prediction of national prominence for the Dallas County Junior College District. The speech follows.

> I wish to express to the people of Dallas County and to the Board of Trustees of its Junior College District my appreciation for the very great honor of being invited to serve as first chief administrator of your junior college district.
>
> Texas will be a new experience for me, and I anticipate that it will be a challenging and satisfying one. Your state is known for the high quality of performance that is demanded of its leaders and public servants. Your trustees have communicated to me this expectation of excellence. I concur completely with this quest for quality and shall concentrate on obtaining it.
>
> Nowhere in the field of education is there more dynamism than in the junior college field. The relatively recent ascendancy of the junior college in American higher education may be attributed to its demonstrated capacity to solve or alleviate some of our most complex contemporary problems—political, social, and economic. Residents of the Dallas area may anticipate that a strong junior college program will provide a comprehensive array of vocational and

professional opportunities for them and their successor generation.

With the public support for junior college education, which is very evident in Dallas, I have every confidence that we will be able to build the Dallas County Junior College District into one of the finest in the nation.[37]

During the next fifteen years the promise and the prediction were fulfilled, but as Priest had noted, Texas was a new experience for him. He knew Texas culture by reputation only. He had never lived in any part of the Bible belt before. It was an anomaly to him that as a routine part of the get acquainted conversation came the question, "What church do you go to?" He soon discovered that agnosticism was equated with atheism in the Dallas area. In his mind, agnostic meant he believed in a supreme being and that the universe was far too complicated a creation for there not to be a God over all. His negative experiences with fanaticism and those taking advantage of others in the name of organized religion caused him to disassociate with formal denominations that seemingly gave human characteristics to God. This explanation was far too complex to explore in casual chit chat. Since he had been reared in the home of his grandfather, an elder in the First Christian Church, Priest had attended those services with him. Based on that history, First Christian became his answer. He lived his life and conducted his business with the moral standards and ethics of Christian teachings. The response was a great simplification of the whole truth, but it avoided the lengthy discourse on whether there was unassailable evidence of the correctness of this or that tenet of one religion or another. Once he was an established member of his personal and professional communities, the question dropped from conversation. His character and life spoke to the issue.[38]

CHAPTER FIVE

Building a National Model
The Flagship

S electing a president was only the first of many tasks facing the newly elected Board of Trustees of the Dallas County Junior College District. At the top of the list was securing a site for the campuses. They chose to wait to involve whoever the president was to be in the land acquisition and planning process. Once Priest had accepted the job, he became the quarterback for the site selections and the planning process for building the seven-college district.[1]

Many factors had led to the decision to establish a multi-college district. The original study for Dallas done by C. C. Colvert had recommended four campuses of forty acres each. The Board of Trustees, however, believed that Dallas never planned big enough and after in-depth studies, they decided to build six campuses with at least two-hundred acres each in outlying areas around the central downtown campus.[2]

There are many issues and concerns associated with a multi-college district, like the debate in 1991 with the Southern Association of Colleges and Schools as whether to accredit each college separately or as a single district. The decision was to continue to accredit each college individually.[3] There are fewer issues with a district comprised of several colleges than with a single college having multiple campuses. In 1965 when that decision was made for Dallas, there were just under twenty multi-college districts in the country. By 1968, that number had grown to forty. Most were established in or close to densely populated areas like Dallas. This growth of junior colleges away from its rural roots to urban areas was attributable to the shift of the population. Rapid changes in technology were calling for education to become more functional in order to answer the needs of the workforce. Addressing the needs of business and industry was the one of the primary missions of the junior college.[4]

Setting up the Dallas system as a multi-college district rather than a multi-campus college would allow each college to reflect the community it served and for each community to feel ownership in its respective college. There has been growth in multi-college districts nationally, but Dallas remains the only one in the south, with the exception of Alamo Community College. Alamo began as a multi-campus college, but then acquired Saint Phillips which was already a free standing institution and needed to retain its identity as a college.[5] Even nationally, most multi-college districts evolved from a single college or small multi-campus colleges, but Dallas began with a specific plan and adequate financing to establish a multi-college district within a short time frame.[6] With most districts, growth required planning differently within an existing system, but the Dallas system began as a whole.[7] The more sites a system has, and the more widespread those locations are, the greater the necessity for separate colleges. Priest's positions in California as president of a new college that absorbed an existing college and then president of a college created by merging two colleges, gave him an experience base for knowing the value of planning a unified system from the beginning.

The separateness of colleges within a district is an organizational structure with less central control than the multi-campus college. This system by design seemed diametrically opposed to the perception of some faculty and administrators in

California, and later in Dallas, that Priest needed absolute control. This perception, like the one of Priest being an autocrat, was not entirely unwarranted. They both related to his awareness of having the ultimate responsibility for all that happened within the college district during his watch. He concurred with those who said there was no autonomy of the colleges even though they were established as separate institutions. Priest was very clear in his definition of autonomy and its existence in any organization. When directly asked about the self-rule of the colleges in an interview in 1994, he replied, "The original answer I gave several years ago to the two division deans that autonomy does not exist is still my answer. Why get into a philosophical discussion about how many angels can fit on a pin head? People who ask a question about autonomy are really asking, 'Will you leave us alone and let us do what we want without your interference?' Hell, no! As soon as I see you're doing it wrong, I'll make you stop. I'm obviously not going to be present in most cases because I am going to have competent people and they are not going to have autonomy because they have a letter that says they have autonomy. They're going to have autonomy because they are doing a damn good job, doing it right, and no intervention is necessary or desirable. It would reduce its effectiveness if you got involved. That is real autonomy." [8]

Priest's definition of autonomy as a competent person doing an excellent job so that no central control was necessary coincided with his belief in the true spirit of individual colleges that reflect their unique communities. As a quantitative representation of that belief, the district office, housed in a central but separate location, had fewer employees and functions during Priest's chancellorship than any time since.[9]

Priest felt at the time the district was established that in a large county like Dallas, the communities to be served by the colleges were substantially different and could not have their needs met with a cookie cutter answer. Operating on the premise of unity with diversity, he believed that the local community should know about the college that served it and the people who worked at that college. It was unimportant for the public to know there was a district chancellor and a downtown office.[10]

The concept of the district office as a holding company overseeing the distribution of educational services allowed each college to be more responsive to the unique needs of each community. Priest also foresaw a better and more valuable accrediting processes if each college was accountable for its own quality. His thought was the Southern Association of Colleges and Schools (SACS) would then have to write specific reports on each college rather than a sweeping overview of the district. This would give each college direct data for improvements without assuming that the SACS Visiting Committee's comments were recommendations for one of the other colleges.

Another advantage of the multi-college structure was that the district became a buffer for the colleges. At the top of a multi-college district, the president or chancellor has four distinct publics to whom he or she must respond: the colleges, the community at-large, the Board of Trustees, and the state. That top position absorbs the responsibility for interaction with the board and the state, freeing the presidents of the colleges to concentrate on their specific communities and colleges. Priest was keenly aware of the importance of responding efficiently and appropriately to all four, never forsaking one to focus sole attention on another.[11]

Priest admitted that overseeing one college was more enjoyable because it allowed for greater involvement with people, but when he came to Dallas the need was great. There was, as he described it, "a major backlog of demand for the types of services a community college can render," so the decision was made to begin with a "massive attack on the problem" by establishing a seven college district to serve the great diversity of needs of Dallas County.[12]

That "massive attack" was a twelve-year task, but several factors in that plan set national standards which were replicated or used as measures for the successful development of other college districts. The DCCCD Master Plan was a comprehensive approach with detailed planning of the entire district's layout before any constructions was begun. From the first phase, all seven colleges were named and a timetable established for construction, including the need for a second bond election in 1972.[13]

Putting seven colleges into operation in twelve years was an achievement noted nationally. In California in the *Bakersfield Scene* newspaper in July of 1976, reporter D. Clemmons wrote, "This is a record unparalleled for a single district in the history of the community college movement regardless of the size of the district."[14] The celerity of the process was only one of the benchmarks achieved by the Dallas board and Priest in building the district's physical plant. Other distinguishing achievements were location and size of each of the properties, parking space philosophy, innovative use of form, and overall aesthetics of the interior and exterior designs.

In October of 1965, the board indicated to Priest that they expected the first college of the district to be opened in September of 1966. Priest hired Deon Holt from the Los Rios College District in California as the director of research and planning to spearhead the implementation of building plans. That allowed only ten months to plan it, build it, set the curriculum, staff it, and open it. It was decided that the renovation of an existing facility might be the most efficient route and that since there would be just one college initially, it should be located in a central area accessible to students from all over Dallas County.[15]

After considering six locations, the site search was narrowed to two: Union Depot and the former Sanger-Harris Department Store complex. The depot offered the advantage of an adjacent parking lot, but the purchase would have to be negotiated through several railroad corporations which could have been a lengthy process. That swung the decision to the former Sanger-Harris complex. The district purchased the site from O. L. Nelms for $2,150,000.[16] The original structure and its extensions were built in the late 1800s by Philip, Elias, Ale, Lehman, Isaac, and Baum Sanger, merchants whose family had immigrated to American from Germany in the 1850s.[17] The store was originally called Sanger Brothers before it purchased and merged with A. Harris department stores. This background of the facility would later give rise to questions of its historical value. Those questions would cost the district time and money for years to come.

With a building selected to house the flagship college of the Dallas district, the task of pulling together all of the things that makes a building a college demanded immediate attention. There had to be a well defined mission and the services and courses to accomplish that mission. In the mid-sixties, the Texas two-year college system was primitive. All of them were junior colleges and operating exactly as that, a junior representation of the senior colleges. They offered the freshman and sophomore years of a four-year degree, had dormitories, and full-blown athletic programs complete with drill teams and cheerleaders. The junior college had a valuable place in higher education, but it was limiting in who it served. Its targeted population was the recent high school graduate seeking a bachelor's degree.[18]

Priest introduced the elements to Dallas that created a comprehensive community college even though the name did not initially reflect that concept. He influenced the board to reject the establishment of a scholarship sports program because it would drain the resources needed for instruction. Priest also brought the concept of emphasizing technical and vocational programs in the curriculum as opposed to relegating these courses to what was commonly called trade schools.[19] This allowed a student to complete a degree or certificate at the two-year college and graduate prepared to enter the work force. Throughout the country, there had been resistance to the inclusion of vocational programs in the junior college offerings. The fear was this would reinforce the class system that had arisen during the industrialization of America by categorizing students as professionals or laborers.[20]

Priest's philosophy and goals for students were on the opposite end of the spectrum from that fear. He stalwartly promoted the dignity of a two-year program and chided the American view that there was some kind of magic in holding a bachelor's degree. On the practical side, he pointed out the economy could not absorb that many people with that level of training. In Priest's words, "The two-year program is designed to prepare people to go out and take their place in civic and family maters," while earning a good income. [21] In fact, time would show that the community college would open the door to higher education for people who were not prepared or confident enough to seek a bachelor's degree.

There was no elitism in Priest's view of the mission of the community college. He saw the transfer degree to a bachelor's degree and the technical/vocational degree as having equal value, each with a vital place in the economy. This philosophy was represented in the physical structure of each of the seven colleges in Dallas. Many states had and still have two-year college systems that housed academic transfer and vocational programs on separate campuses. The DCCCD did not house them in separate buildings unless the size or noise level of equipment necessitated it, such as automotive technology. Priest called the juxtaposition of the academic and technical programs "an attack on social stratification because people working together understand each other."[22]

This same lack of elitism embraced the need for remedial courses. The Dallas colleges would operate with an open door admission policy. The policy stated that anyone over the age of eighteen whose high school class had already graduated would be accepted for college admission. This allowed the enrollment of under-prepared students. To help these students to be successful, the curriculum included various levels of pre-college courses in math, reading, and writing. Even though SAT and ACT courses were not required for entrance into the college, they were collected and assessed to see if the student needed additional testing for their level of preparedness. Priest viewed the community college as a people's college meaning that not every student would arrive fully prepared to tackle a college level curriculum and that remedial courses, called guided studies, were needed to bridge this educational gap. Priest's advocacy for remedial courses at the college level was an indication of his understanding of the non-traditional student that would be a major portion of the students served by community colleges. In a newspaper article published in May, 1966, before El Centro was scheduled to open that fall, Priest explained, "A mature person who missed out on a high school diploma may have the capability of a college education. Through what we call our guided studies program, such students will be able to take remedial courses—English and math for example —to help fill their gaps."[23]

Priest also brought to Texas the concept of non credit courses, then called community service courses, for non degree seeking students. Most of the courses were less than a semester in length and ranged from social skills, like ballroom dancing, to more practical courses, like Spanish for business and travel, and numerous courses offering an update of technical skills.

With the curriculum philosophy in place, they needed to select the degree programs to be offered at El Centro. Just as site selection had been driven by the economy of time and the accessibility to the entire county, curriculum choices were subject to the constraints of the size of space and the fact it was a multi-story building located downtown. Another consideration was county-wide needs of industry and business. Although there were needs for manufacturing related jobs like welding and auto body repair, the downtown high-rise building did not lend itself to the laboratory requirements for such programs.[23]

Al Phillips, newly hired vice president of instruction, and Priest met with area employers to research and identify the areas of greatest need for program development. With all the limitations of space and city ordinances taken into consideration, thirteen programs were designed to target four main industries: data processing, health, fashion, and food preparation. The vocational programs required core academic courses in mathematics, reading, and writing. These core courses also were part of the transfer curriculum for those students who would later pursue a bachelor's degree.[25]

With the identification of the areas for vocational degrees, one being health, El Centro became the first community college in Texas to offer an associate degree in nursing. Priest had fought the battle in California and adding the program to the downtown allied health programs was a natural. Its success was immediate and continued to grow. With a grant from the Division of Nursing of the U.S. Public

Health Service, the ADN curriculum was tailored to meet the needs of veterans with medical training, but who lacked certification from state agencies. The program granted credits based on competency tests and offered seminars in the differences in the practice of military and civilian medicine. The addition of the med-vet program garnered El Centro's ADN program a note in the Congressional Record in 1972. Senator John Tower remarked, "I commend El Centro College and the very capable leadership of Dr. Bill J. Priest, chancellor, and Dr. Robert Leo, director of social projects for this exciting innovation in the education of veterans and allied health personnel."[26]

A student entering El Centro had thirteen vocational careers and a generic transfer degree from which to choose. The excellent curriculum contained courses to support those who entered the open door but were not ready for college level course work. Students had decisions to make and test scores had to be interpreted about levels of readiness for college courses. It was clear to Priest, students would need guidance in these decisions.

In the mid-sixties, the junior colleges in Texas did not have established counseling centers or even formal faculty advising systems. Priest included counseling as part of the master plan for all seven colleges. He ensured that each college provided this service on a greater scale than had ever been offered before in a community college.[27] A desire for student success was the motivation for Priest's support of counseling. He wanted each student to leave the community college with a clear direction for their life and the skills to achieve that goal. Publicly and repeatedly Priest voiced his concern that too many students enrolled in the academic transfer program to pursue a bachelor's degree and then they were not able to find meaningful employment, while there were ample good paying jobs in technical fields for well trained skilled people. In an article, "On the Threshold of Greatness," published in the September, 1966, issue of the *Junior College Journal*, Priest blamed society's glorification of a select few professions for setting unrealistic standards of achievement for many students. He wrote, "It is easy to give lip service to the person who is not going to be a brain surgeon or nuclear physicist, but when all is said and done, the focal point of attention all too often seems to be on those professions which are high in status."[28] The need, however, was for approximately seven technicians or paraprofessionals for every professional. But society began planting the idea in young minds at the elementary school level that only professional jobs requiring a bachelor's degree or more were appropriate goals.[29]

Herein lay the value of counseling; it could offset limited and often inappropriate goals. Initially, the counselor would assist the student in finding a suitable level of study through assessment of current skills. Using evaluations through career interest instruments and discussions, a counselor could guide a student toward a major where there was viable employment, and that would be in line with their aptitude and interests.[30]

The first dean of students at El Centro College, Don Creamer, was impressed with Priest's strong advocacy for counseling as an essential element in the educational process. Creamer recalled the words of Priest in a faculty meeting after it was rumored that there had been complaints about counseling, "Any faculty member who bad mouths counseling is committing a sin worse than ax murder. If I ever learn that a faculty member is bad mouthing counseling, I personally will fire him."[31] Creamer indicated that Priest's powerful support of the counseling function did not stop with words. He made funds available in the budget to hire necessary staff based on Creamer's judgment.

El Centro employed the largest number of certified counselors of any higher education institution in Dallas County or any two-year college in Texas. In fact, the entire student services area had a higher staff to student ratio than most colleges in the country. The first president of El Centro, Don Rippey, concurred that the services of the Learning Resource Center and counseling were of the highest priority. Funding was provided from the general budget with additional dollars from the state for technical and vocational counselors. Priest believed that since students generated part of the revenue through tuition, and purchases in the bookstore and cafeteria, that they should share in the profits. Food service and the bookstore were lease services, with contracts written so that a percent of sales went into funds allocated for student services. Both of those operations reported to the dean of students.[32]

Though his belief in the service was strong, so was his expectation for excellent outcomes in retention and completion rates. These statistics theoretically demonstrated students had been advised into the appropriate levels of courses. Priest set high standards of accountability in every aspect of services and instruction.

These high standards included his creating an environment for innovation and expansion. He was a risk taker and wanted college staff to be risk takers too. Creamer remembered it as almost a demand for innovation and so they tried things that were successful and some things that were not. Eventually the innovations expanded student services to the broader concept of student development. The founding administrators of El Centro established a self-assessment laboratory for initial academic advising. The self-assessment was part of the initial intake process and assisted in directing students into college level or pre-college level courses.[33]

Another unique approach to improving student success was the alignment of counseling concepts with academic content which formulated the first human development courses.[34] Priest was supportive of the new approach to counseling through an instructional format. The human development curriculum was created to deal with the student as a whole person. Most students do not arrive at a community college free of any concern, full of confidence and highly motivated to learn. Priest had spoken to this issue many times. The El Centro student services staff responded with the creative solution of courses that developed the person, and were not limited to providing a knowledge base in a specific area of study. In an interview in 1994, Creamer explained these courses as a "response to the multiple conditions people brought with them to college that handicapped their ability to make the most of their learning opportunities."[35] These human development courses embodied Priest's educational philosophy of teaching the whole student. He stated the mission of the community college, "is to use our resources to help a person be better than they are and get as close as they can to where they want to go, and also to hold up aspirations so they have a better consciousness of what their options are. . . . It is obvious that education does not mean learning work or learning intelligent living; rather learning an intelligent plan of life that includes work, fulfillment, and realization."[36]

This philosophy reflected through the innovations in student services, as well as the overall organization and operation, brought national attention to El Centro College and the burgeoning Dallas County Community College District. There was a steady stream of visitors from all over the country. They came, not only from two-year colleges, but also from the universities. A university in Bakersfield, California heard about the downtown campus and its new and innovative approaches. They sent a contingent to study the utilization of a downtown campus.[37] The newly forming Dallas system was creating national trends in student services, many of which are found as established modes of practice today.[38]

Public acclaim spotlighted the new college on a national level. The U.S. Office of Education issued a report in 1969 lauding El Centro as potentially "the most successful urban college in the nation."[39] The Office of Education's evaluation team enumerated the college's strengths as a stimulating learning environment, close student and faculty contact, the visionary leadership of Bill Priest, and the generous commitment of resources from Dallas constituents. The report was made public in an article in *Southwest Scene Magazine* in the *Dallas Morning News* in 1971.

The value of the entrance and enrollment process established by El Centro and subsequently used by all of the Dallas County colleges was recognized statewide in 1987. Priest had been retired for six years when the Texas State Legislature appointed an education review committee. The focus was on kindergarten though twelfth grade, but the findings had implications for higher education. The committee's report indicated a large percentage of high school graduates were not prepared for freshman college level courses. Most of the institutions of higher education did not have assessment tools in place with remedial courses available for those who did not test at college level readiness in reading, writing, and math. In the fall of 1989, the state implemented Texas Assessment Skills Program (TASP.) An assessment of those three basic skill areas already was being used by the colleges of the DCCCD. Students not passing TASP or a portion of it were required to take remedial courses in the subject area(s) failed.

TASP was a Texas State requirement until August 2003. Through the years, the state allowed a variety of exceptions to TASP testing for colleges with a proven assessment test and successful placement of first-time-in-college students. The Higher Education Coordinating Board and Texas State Legislature's call for the need of a statewide assessment of basic skills for all entering freshmen, supported by remedial courses, validated what the DCCCD had been doing from its beginning in 1966.

The additional services and courses offered by El Centro and each DCCCD college as it opened, required additional staff. In the area of staffing, as with everything else, a premium was placed on excellence. The stress on hiring the best possible faculty, administrators, and staff was not a philosophy imposed on Priest by the Dallas Junior College Board of Trustees. It was a value by which he had always executed that part of his administrative duties. He knew that quality personnel was essential to running a quality institution of higher learning. Had the Dallas Board of Trustees not shared that belief, and supported it with an adequate budget, Priest would not have accepted the position. In an article in the *Sacramento Union* while Priest was president of American River College, he was asked about the importance of hiring the right personnel. Priest replied, "Pull out the stops in assembling a good faculty. Faculty is the lifeblood of your college. Unusually able people will attract other able people. Mediocre personnel will earmark your operation as mediocre, and it will be difficult or impossible to undo the initial faux pas."[40] Bob Thornton had assured Priest that conserving money was not the objective in hiring decisions. In an interview in 1975, Thornton recalled what he had said to Priest, "We cannot ask you to come here and to create a brand new something and then tie your hands as to the tools you can use, and the tools are going to be your lieutenants. . . . Pay what it takes to get what you want."[41] That set the confirmed goal of hiring the "top grade" instructors and administrators.

Priest officially took the helm as president of the Dallas County Junior College District in October of 1965 and he immediately made his first three personnel recommendations: Alfred M. Phillips, for vice president of instruction; Frank P. Schroeter, for special assistant for planning and research; and Carol Zion, as associate dean of instruction. Phillips came from Moses Lake College in Washington. Schroeter was from the Office of School Planning in Minnesota, and Zion came from Miami Dade Community College in Florida. All three were approved at the November board meeting.[42]

The selection of the person for the top position of El Centro was as important as those who would make district-wide decisions. The criteria was clear-cut. They needed someone who had top level experience in a two-year college and a good track record. The person would need to be able to do an excellent job efficiently, be able to readily recognize problems, and know what to do to remedy them. The job was a very good opportunity and if it were opened to a national search, they were assured of getting a high number of applicants, some of whom would be able to take on the task at hand. Time was of the essence and the feeling was that collectively this new administrative staff had the network and the wherewithal to assess and hire quickly.

Phillips recommended a colleague from Washington, Don Rippey, who was the president of Pasco Junior College at the time. They brought him in for an interview. He had opened a college, was articulate, and was serious about quality education. Priest extended the offer and Rippey agreed to be in Dallas and ready to work in thirty days.[43]

In the all-out effort to open El Centro College by August, 1966, personnel appointments were approved at virtually every board meeting. While an incredibly short time line was a driving factor, the board never questioned Priest's recommendations. There was unified trust in his ability. According to Margaret McDermott, the feeling was that Priest had "a real knack for selecting the right person."[44] That sense of his skill to read people would prove to be right repeatedly through the years as he selected people from unlikely backgrounds for jobs he believed they could do. One of the first was the hiring of Deon Holt, a journalist, to plan and oversee the building of the campuses.

Priest's hiring skills were not limited to selecting the right people. He was also very good at recruitment. Priest set-up interview sessions in various parts of the country, scheduling several interview times and dates per each location. He chose to go to cold snowy areas during the peak of winter. He had a carrousel slide show for them to watch while candidates were sitting in an outer room waiting for an interview. The slides were of sunny lake shores, boating, golf courses, and all things warm and wonderful in Texas. The choices were then his because the candidates were already sold on the move.[45]

Quality checks must go beyond the initial hiring process. Paying well for master teachers and the best administrators implies an expectation of high performance. Priest instigated continuous quality controls from evaluation of all personnel to involving faculty in the decision-making process for shared governance and a system of checks and balance.[46]

The structure established for faculty gave no rank. All faculty members were peers with one title of instructor rather than a hierarchy of titles. The salary structure for faculty was based on the number of years of experience and degrees earned, but no college titles came with that variance. There was no tenure. A three-year contract was the longest time of assured employment and was part of the evaluation process.[47] Gayle Weaver, the first faculty association president, said faculty members preferred the three-year contract to the initial proposal of a five-year contract. It permitted a division dean to deal with a poor performer by allowing the contract to wind down without offer of another. At the end of each year, the dean could review and discuss areas of needed improvement that must be accomplished to earn another three-year contract. A good review gave an instructor a new three-year contract at the end of each year. The stepping down to the end of a three-year contract was instigated only when an instructor had breached professional ethics and needed to improve in order to continue employment in the DCCCD. It was also a form of protection for the instructor. A dean could not dismiss a faculty member based on one year's poor evaluation.[48]

That system of evaluation for instructors involved evaluation forms filled out by students, classroom visits by the division dean, and a set of criteria developed by the faculty association. Priest was emphatic about the quality of teaching being measurable without infringement on academic freedom. C. Parsons quoted Priest in an article in 1966 in the *Christian Science Monitor* on the definition of teaching. Priest said, "Teaching is too important to be exempted from measurement. Any admission that we can't tell good teaching from bad teaching is an admission that we're hopelessly confused."[49] He was also one of the strongest advocates of faculty rights.

When Priest came to Dallas, he established the first faculty association for a community college in the state of Texas.[50] Although there was not an official school of management at that time, called total quality management, Priest was a forerunner of that philosophy. He sought input and encouraged decisions to be made at the lowest level "by the doer," predicated on the belief it was better to have an administrative request for faculty to form an association than to wait for an issue that would rally the faculty into an association.[51] Priest set forth the charge to the El Centro College faculty to form an association. He believed that faculty input was essential in all areas related to academics. He also believed the faculty association president should have direct access to the top person in the college, which in this case was him. He called it "dependent pragmatism" in that any complaint or criticism from faculty association officers was worthy of investigation even if they were reported to be perpetual complainers.[52] Reflecting back over the years at the time of his retirement in 1981, Priest said even those occasional association officers who were not constructive in their leadership approach kept the organization vital and moving.

Priest's sincere advocacy for faculty was proven early on. One of the first efforts on the part of the newly formed faculty association was to present Priest with a salary proposal. He promptly told them it was not high enough and sent them away to write another. Gayle Weaver, association president at the time, recalled, "Priest beat the hell out of our proposal asking for a four-hundred-dollar a year raise. He said our data were out of date and inaccurate. Then he reached in a file and pulled out more current information, and handed it to us. He charged us with writing a new proposal and encouraged us to ask for eight-hundred-dollars a year." [53] The motivation behind that response was Priest's desire to continue to try to recruit the best teachers for the rapidly growing district. In order to do that, he wanted the salaries to be more competitive. He also wanted the salaries to be a factor in drawing skilled staff until the new Dallas system had time to develop a reputation that would be the enticement. Indeed, the salaries and the reputation of the DCCCD being a quality place to work did attract top instructors. The year before Priest retired, the Dallas County Community College District boasted well over one-third of its academic faculty held a Ph.D., compared to the national average of one-fifth.[54]

While the benefits designed for administrators did not include the same protections of an association or a three-year contract as provided to faculty, it was an attractive package. Again, he built on a philosophy he had formulated and publicly spoken about in previous leadership positions. In a 1962 article published in the *Junior College Journal*, Priest advised new presidents to set-up organizations with "clear-cut job specifications, unambiguous echelon relationships, and well-defined guiding principles and regulations." [55] The district office provided generic job descriptions for each administrative position that could be adapted to the needs of each college. There was a good salary schedule, unparalleled opportunity for upward mobility, and a generous sick-leave and vacation policy. Priest realized the stresses of a twelve month a year job that often demanded more than the usual forty hours of work in a week would require adequate time for vacation and renewal. Administrators earned enough vacation to enable them to take one week every three months if that is how they chose to use it.

This was not a simple perk, but a sincere belief Priest had in the need for professional rejuvenation.[56]

All of his principles of management were evidenced during his tenure as president of the American Association of Junior Colleges' board. He was elected to the role in 1966 and while working feverishly to open a new college and inaugurate a college district, Priest gave substantial attention to AAJC. Ed Gleazer, who was the executive director at the time remembers Priest as "a productive partner."[57] Priest directed the AAJC in drafting personnel policies and salary schedules for staff, and worked to improve the position of the executive director's position. He worked with the board to raise the position's salary to a level comparable to a community college president of a metropolitan institution. He also initiated approval of a leave of absence for the executive director every three years for a period of two months that could be added to the annual one month vacation. It would not only allow a time for renewal, but also the opportunity to pursue other projects of personal or professional growth.[58]

There is considerable evidence that Priest respected those who worked for him as people who had lives outside work, and who would benefit in time away from work. His detractors sometimes painted a picture of a myopic work-focused, rule-enforcing Captain Bligh, but the words of most of those who worked for him and his actions counter that description.

In his capacity as President of AAJC, Priest worked diligently to bring all junior colleges to the table to work together. In his keynote address the AAJC national convention Priest called for the forming of an "Academy of Junior College Education." This was not in conflict with the functions of the association. AAJC was the national lobbying arm of the two-year colleges fighting for their fair share of federal support through bills and funding. The academy envisioned by Priest would provide a clearing house for sharing best practices and encourage the development of new ideas. In the speech, he explained that the junior college movement had matured, but the junior and community colleges had not reached full development. There would be benefit in bringing together leaders who had contributed significantly to the growth and development of junior colleges for study of what was in place and of new directions.[59] The speech, "On the Threshold of Greatness," was published in the *American Association of Junior Colleges Journal* reaching a wider audience than just those in attendance at the convention.

In 1967, B. Lamar Johnson, a professor in higher education at the University of California at Los Angeles, invited a select group of junior and community college presidents to form just such an organization. Even though the Dallas County Junior College District was only a year old and had only one college in operation, Priest's invitation to participate was based on the fact he was already recognized as a national leader in two-year education and El Centro had already set a standard as a national model in the areas of counseling and developmental studies.

Rather than the term of "academy" that Priest had used, the organization became the League for Innovation. It was officially founded in 1968 and Johnson was the founding Executive Director but served only in a part-time capacity. In a relatively short time it was determined that a full-time director was needed.[60] Terry O'Banion was selected to be the first full-time executive director. Priest chaired the hiring committee and was initially put off by O'Banion's rather free-spirit demeanor. He knew O'Banion had the experience necessary: he was then a professor at the University of Illinois, he had worked in fund raising, and also as a dean in a community college. During the interview, O'Banion revealed himself to be astute and savvy about higher education issues and the important place of two-year colleges. The League for Innovation under O'Banion's leadership proved to be a valuable asset to the community college movement.[61]

The attitude of always seeking new solutions and taking risks seemed to be an innate part of Priest. His basic nature was the springboard for his behavior and management philosophy. In his job as President of American River College in 1959, Priest wrote an article about the problems facing this new entity in higher education. He wrote, "The absence of universally accepted 'ground rules' assures an experimental attitude in operational situations, which is certain to produce a continuous flow of better answers to many problems being dealt with throughout the nation."[62] This implied that necessity was the mother of innovation, but Priest's drive for betterment went far beyond the need to solve problems.

He had absolute intolerance for those who had become too comfortable with the status quo. He saw education as being in a state of transition and demanding more than sacred, time-tested routes to traditional ends. There were faculty members who held strong to the belief in the intrinsic value of education for the ethereal sake of education. Priest insisted that more pragmatic approaches were necessary for pragmatic results. He knew that two-year colleges were not miniature universities filled with new high school graduates headed toward a bachelor's degree. Many community college students were lacking a high school diploma or had several intervening years since graduation; their motivation for attending college was to acquire marketable skills to get a good job. For some that would require transferring to a four-year institution and pursuing a bachelor's degree. For a high percentage that would entail earning a certificate or an associate's degree in a technical or vocational field. Priest chided faculty and administrators who resisted these changing demographics. The battle was not quickly won. Almost ten years later in an article in the *Dallas Morning News* on the value of higher education, Priest described the raw process of change as these resisters "were kicking and screaming and being dragged into the world of reality" by daily experiences on campus.[63]

Another reality resisted by the majority of the academic community was marketing, the need to get word out to the public about the college and what it had to offer. In the mid-sixties, marketing was not the popular term—there was sales and there was public relations. Both were viewed by most in higher education as slick presentations of mostly hype to solicit favor and money on products or services. Academicians felt it was demeaning to education to use such methods. Education had intrinsic value and did not need to be "sold."[64] Through formal course work and experience, Priest knew that both sales and public relations were essential to having a well attended and respected college. Certainly, the strongest marketing tool is a legion of successful graduates who, by excellent performances in the workplace and by their own expressions of their satisfaction with the junior college experiences, represent and promote the community college. Word-of-mouth has always been and still is the best form of marketing, but it is limited and slow and is only one aspect of a total marketing program.

Priest's grasp of the fundamental value of marketing as a critical element of the success of a college and in the positive progress of the community college movement, gave him an extra dimension in his leadership role of president of the Dallas Junior College District. He saw public relations as a necessity for institutional success in maintaining a positive image with the community and news media. He understood the need to "sell" by letting the public know the courses, degrees, and services that were available to them. He knew the importance of every aspect from internal marketing to external target market research.[65]

The importance of public relations was the focus of an article Priest wrote in the early 1950s. He advised junior college presidents to survey the community for needs and expectations, and to develop good media relations by maintaining an accurate flow of information externally and internally. He further advised them to create collateral material to augment what was done by the media.[66]

Priest was so delighted with the supportive media, both print and electronic, he found in Dallas because he knew how powerful the media was in influencing public opinion. The media was equally delighted with him because he appreciated them and kept them informed. He knew how to use them in that he was well aware of what they should not be used for. According to thirty-year television news veteran, John Whitson, the best way to use the news media for positive results is simply to keep them supplied with accurate information, and always to allow them access to whomever they want to interview. He emphasized that nothing makes a reporter more suspicious than being told "no comment" or that a key person is unavailable for comment. Priest created a partnership with the news media. He was always honest and quick to respond, and he appreciated reporters calling him if they "uncovered something."[67]

Priest was among the first junior college leaders in the country to hire a full-time public relations person. Sybil Hamilton, a former member of the Dallas City Council, assisted him with keeping the media informed, producing promotional materials, and working with the Texas State Legislature on educational issues. The approach to public relations was not the glitz and glitter reviled by educators, but one of providing a steady flow of accurate and honest information whether in a press release, brochure, or statistics for the legislature. Priest was so insistent on accuracy that Hamilton once sent him a picture of himself taken when he accepted the Dallas position with a note paper clipped to it, "You need a new picture. This one has too much hair." He had a new picture made. He had to be true to his external market.[68]

Throughout his tenure as chancellor, Priest kept the person in the role of public relations for the district in the inner circle and part of the information loop. Public relation directors were not viewed by Priest as feature writers, but as intelligent professionals who had a great deal to contribute to the organization. He realized it was essential for that person to be up to speed on the happenings, good or bad, that were going on in the district in order for them to respond knowledgably to questions from the press. At his retirement, he thanked then DCCCD Director Claudia Robinson and all of the campus directors of public information for having made improvements in spreading the word of the colleges' "manpower development capabilities."[69] The development of a campus position in public information was directly attributable to Priest's erudition of marketing's place in the success of a college.

As for the internal market, Priest tried to keep a clear downward flow of information. He knew the importance of two-way communication for high morale and effective management. The most important internal market was the Board of Trustees. Terry O'Banion, long term executive director of the League for Innovation said that Priest set a national precedent in the governance model established with the Dallas board. Priest's speeches, writings and interviews are filled with laudation for the Dallas County Community College Board and are replete with points on the importance of open communication lines and positive working relationship any chief executive officer must maintain with the Board of Directors/Trustees. Priest's acumen on board relations put in place a governance model unique to most educational institutions. In 1995, "The Carver Model of Governance" was published and followed by many college boards including the DCCCD board. That model outlined the unwritten philosophy under which Priest and the early Dallas boards functioned. Its tenants are simple: the board sets policy, they deal with the chancellor, and the chancellor handles the rest. That is soundly in place today.

The one aspect in which this has changed is directly related to the Texas Open Meetings Law. In those first years, there were private pre-meeting meetings usually held over dinner at the Dallas Club. In the words of the first board chair, Bob Thornton, "When we went into the formal meeting we'd already had our bloodletting."[70] Even with the end of those pre-meetings, the telephone calls continued. Priest had made a practice of sending a printed agenda of the forthcoming meeting to each board member with a personal cover memorandum explaining items that needed additional data for clear understanding. When there was an item that he knew was of particular concern to a trustee, he would give a heads-up call to answer questions or provide additional information. Likewise, board members called Priest if they had questions or real reservations on an issue. They would ask for information beforehand, rather than taking the time in the public meetings. It was a system that worked well for the board and for the college district.[71]

Priest used an expression, "the care and feeding of board members." It sounded condescending or sarcastic at best, but it was pure in its oversimplification of the principles of good communication and good working relationships. Priest said he almost had Bob Thornton convinced to co-author an article by that title. Priest explained the phrase as "very close to the top in importance of anything a chief administrator does. A leader must be able to see from the window of each board member and must address it. Admit to your sins. Be thoughtful. Be considerate. Make a simple telephone call before meetings to prepare them. There should be no surprises. Let them know if one of your recommendations is going to be in opposition to their view. Solicit their support. Is that political? Yes, but it's good politics. It's communication."[72] He was always well researched in matters to be presented at the meetings. In his fifteen-year tenure with the DCCCD, not one of Priest's recommendations was ever voted down; most passed unanimously.[73] There were times when the amount of discussion seemed to indicate that more research was necessary. At that point, Priest would ask to withdraw the item from the agenda and to table it for further study.[74]

It was that genuine enthusiasm of the original board for the task at hand that was of prime importance in Priest's decision to accept the Dallas job. He had been enticed by the idea of working with people who wanted what he wanted. That speculation proved to be true. The first board members were fantastic logistical providers. Priest recalled, "I never had to worry about if they would be there. I didn't have to spend sixty percent of my time feeding them information. They asked, 'What can we do to get it done?' and it was done."[75] He attributes the success of the DCCCD to the Board of Trustees.

That admiration of Priest for the board was mutual and expressed often and publicly. In 1971, Thornton was quoted in *Dallas Scene Magazine*, "When you have an administration you have great respect for, you don't have any thorny problems."[76] Ten years later, then board member Robert Powers echoed that sentiment in an article in *D Magazine*, "From public experience, I never dealt with anybody like Bill Priest in terms of candor, ability, and following his goal of making this the best district."[77]

The greatest demonstration of respect and trust was represented in the latitude the board gave to Priest. From the onset, Thornton publicly stated the faith the board had in him. He said the trustees were unanimous in their support to give Priest direct responsibility and authority to do his job without continually seeking a vote.[78]

That first board was in one accord and seemingly singular in mind, perhaps because they were all on the ground floor in beginning this new educational venture for the citizens of Dallas County. In New Guinea's Pidgin language there is a word, *wanbel*. It means of one mind for one goal. That is the way the first board functioned. It was so utopian, even Priest questioned its reality. Priest dealt most often with the board chair. He wondered if he were somehow being inappropriate or making the other members feel excluded. He queried one of the Trustees about protocol. The board member reassured him that if ever there was disagreement or dissatisfaction that it would be expressed. Each member felt free to call Priest directly. He further explained why Thornton was so confidently given the lead by the other Trustees by offering an analogy, "If you want to win the Kentucky Derby, you don't get a plow horse."[79] Thornton was a paragon of accomplishment.

This efficient and successful, albeit somewhat guarded, form of doing business brought public criticism from a local magazine the year before Priest announced his retirement. The article in *D Magazine* referred to the governance of the DCCCD as "old-style Dallas politics." The article further condemned the district by saying, "The community college district has escaped democracy. It is the last Dallas public institution to be dominated by the business community."[80] In that article, Bill Bancroft quoted Priest's defense of the system by attributing the "placid relationship as one of the key ingredients in successfully building a quality community college system." Priest further explained that if it was necessary "to make waves" in order to get to an important target and accomplish what needed to be done, then that was what would have been done. He stressed that agreement should not garner "negative brownie points." The article also pointed critically to low voter turnout for board elections. Priest indicated the lack of involvement from the populace was tantamount to a vote of confidence in the status quo.[81]

Margaret McDermott summed up the success of the working relationships of the board and Priest in a more personal way. She said there was mutual support for each other in the work at hand that resulted in friendships. She acknowledged there were disagreements, but they worked them through. One of the elements that kept those disagreements from erupting into public power plays was lack of egotism. Priest's ego was tied to the success of the college district as a whole, not who individually received credit for it. The board members did not need to exhibit egos in their jobs as trustees because they had earned their stature elsewhere and felt no need to make power plays within the workings of the district.[82] This was confirmed by 1980s board chair, Jerry Gilmore as quoted in *D Magazine*, "This has not been a place for political 'showboatism' or a platform for personal ambitions."[83]

The leadership of Dallas County determined that a community college was the right direction for higher education in the fast growing county, even though the concept was new and somewhat undefined. Don Rippey, the first president of El Centro College, credited "the Dallas power structure" for having the wisdom to broaden the base of accessible education beyond one that only benefits the elite. The development of a downtown college first broadened the constituency by being convenient to those who worked downtown, and being accessible by public transportation. In establishing its content of courses and services, the philosophy and organizational structure was in place for the addition of the other six colleges to locate a campus within twenty minutes drive time of anyone living or working in Dallas County.

This old tintype pictures Priest's beloved maternal grandmother, Adah Freeman Stubbs, *(standing)* with her sister, Clara Freeman, who was a medical doctor, a rare achievement for a woman in the early 1900s. Priest's grandmother was one of the most positive influences in his formative years.

Decked out in full uniform, four-year old Priest takes a determined stance even though he is wielding a broken bat held together with tape.

Priest earned all three of his degrees from the University of California at Berkeley. This snapshot was taken of Priest on campus in the spring of 1935 when he was a freshman.

A Berkeley student photographer had Priest take a dramatic spread-eagle
stance—completely inappropriate for a baseball pitcher, but the artistry
made an eye-catching promotional picture.

The promotional photographs in the professional leagues had more of a Hollywood star mystique. Priest, like all players on the Philadelphia Athletics ball club, had a signed photo to give fans.

On an intelligence mission to Mindanao, Philippines during World War II, the small plane had to be landed on a dirt road. Priest *(left)* and the other officer immediately were surrounded by the Filipinos.

Priest *(left)* is standing in front of the Manila Hotel, which had been occupied by the enemy. American Marines took the hotel room by room, tossing in a grenade and then checking for survivors.

In dress uniform in 1941, Priest struck a pose with a cigar imitating Winston Churchill. Priest never smoked. Both of his parents had been heavy smokers, which repulsed him.

Shortly after arriving in Dallas in 1965, the demand for "official portraits" began. This was one of his first. Courtesy Dallas County Community College District Archives, District Service Center

This is the first Board of Trustees and Chancellor of the Dallas County Community College District, the people who took a goal of providing a convenient, inexpensive, quality college education to all of the citizens of Dallas County and made it a reality. Seated in the front row *(from left to right)* are R. L. Thornton, Jr., Margaret McDermott, and Bill Priest. Standing on the back row *(from left to right)* are Durwood Sutton, Loncy Leake, Frank Altick, Franklin Spafford, and Carrie Welch. Courtesy Dallas County Community College District Archives, District Service Center

The exterior of the Sanger Brothers Department Store building remained undisturbed when the interior was renovated to house El Centro College, which opened in the fall of 1966. Courtesy Dallas County Community College District Archives, District Service Center

There had been so much controversy over the structural soundness of the old Sanger Brothers building that some El Centro employees enjoyed exaggerating the lack of safety in staff offices. Courtesy Dallas County Community College District Archives, District Service Center

Bill Priest *(center)* accepts a scholarship check for Dallas County Junior College students from Durwood J. Tucker, Managing Director of WRR Radio *(left)* and W. H. Roberts, Executive Vice President of American Bank and Trust *(right)*, circa 1969. The DCCCD continues to be the recipient of financial gifts from business and industry, as evidenced in the successful Rising Star Scholarship program funded entirely by private donations. The fund was the concept of R. L. Thornton, III, Chairman of the DCCCD Foundation Board. Courtesy Dallas County Community College District Archives, District Service Center

Eastfield College was an impressive structure on the Mesquite landscape in 1970. Today the view is obscured by the vestiges of a growing population including R. L. Thornton Freeway on the east side of the campus. Courtesy Dallas County Community College District Archives, District Service Center

Mountain View College in southwest Oak Cliff opened on schedule albeit with some classes and offices in trailers. Courtesy Dallas County Community College District Archives, District Service Center

Inspired by the design of North Park Mall, Mountain View's contiguous structure is surrounded by man-made ponds, fountains, and a natural creek and foliage. Courtesy Dallas County Community College District Archives, District Service Center

Richland College on the boundary of Dallas and Richardson in far north Dallas County consistently boasts the highest enrollment in the DCCCD. Courtesy Dallas County Community College District Archives, District Service Center

Located in Irving in west Dallas County, North Lake was carved into the rolling terrain giving it an intriguing multilevel structure. It opened simultaneously with Cedar Valley College in 1977. Courtesy Dallas County Community College District Archives, District Service Center

Cedar Valley is in Lancaster in south Dallas County. The buildings are standard rectangles with only a few dramatic architectural lines. Courtesy Dallas County Community College District Archives, District Service Center

Cedar Valley draws its beauty from the lake and carefully planned landscaping. Courtesy Dallas County Community College District Archives, District Service Center

Each college had a dedication ceremony and reception for the community it served shortly after the official opening. The next to the last such ceremony was held at Cedar Valley in the arena theatre. By then, the Board of Trustees had changed by two. In the front row *(from left to right)* are Trustee Robert Powers, Trustee Carrie Welch, Vice Chancellor Walter Pike, Trustee Margaret McDermott, CVC President Floyd Elkins, Trustee Loncy Leake, Chancellor Bill Priest, and Trustee Pattie Powell. In the back row *(from left to right)* are Trustee Durwood Sutton, Vice Chancellor Deon Holt, Vice Chancellor Jan LeCroy, and Trustee R. L. Thornton, Jr. Courtesy Dallas County Community College District Archives, District Service Center

The infamous and bladeless windmill loomed above the Brookhaven campus for many years before being dismantled in 1984. Deon Holt, the first president of Brookhaven, believes it was ahead of its time and that with the technology available today it would work. Courtesy Dallas County Community College District Archives, District Service Center

Marietta and Bill Priest attended many District and College functions. In this photo circa 1980, they were visiting with Carol Schlipak *(center)*, the first director of the DCCCD Foundation.

Dale Parnell, Executive President of the American Association of Community and Junior Colleges, gave Priest this picture taken as he delivered a speech at the national AACJC convention. Parnell's message credited Priest with Harry Truman-like characteristics.

During Priest's tenure as chancellor in the DCCCD, he was given many tributes. His appreciation of fine wine was well known. The lead instructor in the El Centro Culinary Arts Degree program, Gus Katsigris, made an eloquent speech and then caught Priest off-guard with the presentation of a bottle of very cheap wine.

Priest loved fishing. In 1988, he negotiated a guided fishing trip in Alaska as payment for a commencement address. He caught a forty-four-pound King Salmon.

In 1991, Priest went hunting in Alberta, Canada. He shot the quota of Greater Canada geese. Each member of the hunting party had his picture taken with the group's total game.

Bill and Ann Priest at a social function in 1997.

Eighteen years after his retirement, Priest was still highly sought as a speaker. Here, he is addressing the 1999 League for Innovation Conference.

In thirty-seven years, the DCCCD had only four chancellors. Pictured here *(from left to right)* are Larry Tyree (1988–1990), Bill Priest (1965–1981), Bill Wenrich (1991–2003), and Jan LeCroy (1981–1987).

On August 1, 2003, Jesus Carreon became the fifth chancellor of the DCCCD. Courtesy Scott Keith (photographer) and Jesus Carreon.

The only picture of Priest and this biographer together was taken at his eightieth birthday party held at the City Club atop One Main Place in downtown Dallas. Pictured *(from left to right)* are Colin Shaw, who worked in the District Office in the 1980s, John Whitson, Bill Priest, and Kathleen Whitson, biographer.

It was a first for all four Executive Presidents of the American Association of Community Colleges to be present at one event. The occasion was a program of the newly formed Bill J. Priest Center for Community College Education of the University of North Texas, held in February 2001 for the 100th Anniversary of Community Colleges. Steve Katsinas, Buchholtz Endowed Chair of the UNT Center, coordinated the event. Pictured *(from left to right)* are Bill Priest, George Boggs (current President), Ed Gleazer (1958–1981), Dale Parnell (1981–1991), and David Pierce (1991–2000).

On vacation in California, Ann Priest's grandchildren stopped at the site where Priest had spent his childhood. They had their picture made under the street sign honoring the family name of their new grandfather.

The Administration Building at American River Junior College in Sacramento, California, was built in 1956. It was named for Priest when he left in 1965.

The Bill J. Priest Institute for Economic Development in the Dallas County Community College District was constructed and named for Priest in 1987.

CHAPTER SIX

Building a National Model
And Then There Were Seven

E l Centro opened the fall semester of 1966 with all the essential elements in place and an enrollment of 4,047 students. That was 2,047 more than had been projected.[1] It was a success. That October, Priest marked one year with the Dallas County Community College District. Thornton asked Priest how much he wanted for a raise. Priest thanked him for the offer and vote of confidence it implied, but he told Thornton he thought it was premature. Priest explained that the first year of operation and continuing progress in the development of the college district would be the true indicator of his deserving a raise. Priest "walked his talk" and expected to be evaluated and held to the same standards by his supervisors that he used in the evaluation of those who reported to him. He had asked for a healthy salary and benefits package when he was hired, but it was one he believed to be fair to himself and to the budget of the new college district. In October of 1967, Thornton again approached Priest with the question of the amount of a raise. The year had been successful; El Centro's enrollment was growing and plans were moving forward for the other colleges. Priest asked for ten-thousand-dollars and the Board of Trustees agreed.[2]

The plans for the other six colleges included selecting the sites. The general area for each college had been charted in the earliest planning stages. Names for all seven colleges were decided at that time as well. The board was besieged with proposals from groups all over Dallas County. Several factors were considered in choosing the land and locations for each campus. Not the least of these was Priest's promise to the North Dallas Chamber of Commerce that every citizen in Dallas County would be no farther than twenty minutes away from a Dallas County Junior College campus.[3] With the traffic levels in the late sixties, that was feasible. The committee operated under the profoundly simple principle that in the purchase of land with taxpayer money, you have to get it right the first time.[4] That meant focusing on quality and accessibility with an eye on the future.

Although the founding of the college district was a response to immediate needs, Priest knew he was planning for future generations. Priest and the board toured existing college campuses all over the country to get ideas. They would gather the best concepts for implementation and modification in formulating their own plans. The mistakes in land selection and construction made by other colleges also benefited them by teaching them what to avoid. At this time, all community and junior colleges were growing, but most had no land on which to expand. Some of the colleges had made frugal purchases to get started. Others had initially purchased more land than they needed, but subsequently sold it. They could not respond to the enrollment growth by building new buildings because they lacked the land. The Dallas County Junior College Board of Trustees made a commitment to buy no less than two-hundred acres per campus and not to sell any of the land. They knew that there would be a continued increase in enrollment at the colleges for many years to come because of the unique niche they filled in higher education and because the population of Dallas County was destined to grow.[5]

Adequate parking also called for large land purchases. Community colleges with rare exception were commuter colleges. In 1966, an article by R. Lynes in *Harper's Magazine* stressed that a new junior college could operate with a minimal library and inadequate classrooms, but a parking lot was essential. The plan to scatter the campuses throughout Dallas County guaranteed they would not be served by public transportation. The city of Dallas had a transit system at the time, but it did not serve the outlying areas. As buildings were added, parking space would have to follow. It was a farsighted decision to make each college campus no less than two-hundred acres regardless of the expectations of initial enrollments. Priest and the board also decided the parking should be free without reserved spaces for faculty, administrators or staff. Priest believed in an egalitarian parking system. It was a message to students that they were important.[6]

The only inequity in parking arrangements existed at El Centro College. While it was accessible by public transportation, those who drove a car had to pay for parking in a commercial lot. This was true for employees and students alike. There was no land to purchase in downtown Dallas for a parking lot. The land that was acquired as part of the Sanger's package was designated for buildings. This inequity existed until 1988, when the Board of Trustees voted to give monthly stipends for parking to the employees at El Centro to compensate for the additional expense they incurred for parking at the downtown campus.[7]

Parking was a major consideration in the building of the other six campuses. Eastfield and Mountain View were the next two colleges planned and built. Eastfield's 244 acre site is in Mesquite which is in east Dallas County, and Mountain View's two-hundred acre site is in Oak Cliff in the southwest sector. Oak Cliff is physically part of the city of Dallas, but began as a small town, Hord's Ridge, and was annexed to the city in 1904.[8] Mesquite is a separate municipality adjacent to the city of Dallas. Deon Holt was in charge of the oversight of planning and construction of the new campuses. An Educational Facilities Lab funded by the Ford Foundation made it possible to bring in a consultant, Harold Gore. Frank Schroeter, another consultant, who was a retired planning and development officer from California, was also brought to Dallas. A generous budget allowed the board and staff members to travel to campuses with state-of-the-art designs to inspire innovative thinking.[9] Priest and the board wanted campuses that were distinctive and did not look like replicas of a central office or secondary schools. They also drew from the architectural designs of the newest structures around Dallas. Schroeter saw great potential for a college campus in the layout of Northpark shopping center in north Dallas. It was his observation that a college could function more efficiently housed in a continuous structure that would give a sense of community to all the various departments and services. It would make them more accessible to students than the university model where each program was housed in a separate building. The networked structure would also include the food service area and the bookstore. Like the shopping center, the parking lot would encircle the buildings. Students could park, walk up to the closest entrance, and not have to return outside until the close of their academic day.[10] Mountain View was built on this model, but unlike a shopping mall, there are large windows in some of the halls and the group areas. Student lounges look out on rustic scenes of trees, the diminutive canyon-like rocky landscape, and a creek. Even today on campus, there is a sense of being far from a populated area.

Priest was a believer in innovative but practical use of space. Trustee Margaret McDermott, a respected patron of the arts, stressed aesthetics. The whole board desired unique and excellent campuses. These formed a synergy of creativity and cutting edge designs. Priest saw the value of aesthetics beyond that of being visually pleasing. He saw it as a very subtle but powerful marketing tool of image. He explained, "Cosmetics influence the external public. It seduces them to come see what you have, but then you must have substance behind those pretty walls."[11] He also strongly believed that the structure should represent the community. It was his goal to have the designs inspire pride. "People driving by the place will say, 'Here is an establishment that makes our community a better place,'" were Priest's words in a *Dallas Morning News* article in May, 1966.[12]

The planning climate set by Priest did not allow beauty bereft of educational purpose. It incorporated the concept that form should follow function. Even the mall concept used at Mountain View was intended to stimulate learning. It put on display what was going on. A community member or potential student touring the facility or current students walking to their next destinations could look into labs and be aware of what was taking place in those areas.[13] Such traffic flow could be disruptive, so all the halls were carpeted to alleviate this problem.[14]

Eastfield was built simultaneously with Mountain View in order to broaden the service area more quickly. The parking lots at Eastfield encircled the buildings, but they were not connected in a continuous flow like a shopping mall. The campus was built in an area with established residential dwellings on one side and commercially zoned property on the other. It was imperative that the college be distinctive to these structures and visible from the freeway on the east side of the campus. The individual buildings with their one-sided slanted roof lines were clustered around a large meandering courtyard and when viewed at a distance gave the illusion of one large castle-like configuration.[15]

Both colleges were scheduled to open the fall of 1970. Priest, Holt, and the board had been meticulous in all of the planning, but in the words of poet Robert Burns "The best laid schemes o' mice an' men . . . ." In May of 1970, the Building Trades Union went on strike. No amount of negotiation from college personnel made any headway. This was a union-called strike and the brick layers had to support the union. Priest was a man of action and not afraid of tainting his image. He was more concerned with getting the colleges completed and opened on time. He went to the union hall and talked with the officers of the union. He drew on the vernacular of his days working with his brother-in-law as a stevedore in the shipping yards. He hit the union officers with a barrage of profanity ending with the point that it was "goddamn stupid of you to prevent us from building colleges to educate your kids."[16] He spoke their language, lifted a barrier, and they listened. They seemed to think this educator was an all right guy and that no one had really explained the situation to them before. They agreed to complete the work at Eastfield and Mountain View, but it was not to be public knowledge. The strike continued at other construction sites. Then just one week before the two campuses were to open, striking carpet workers encircled each campus with picket signs. Both colleges opened on schedule albeit with tents and temporary buildings at Mountain View.[17]

With each new campus, a review of possible technical programs occurred and those decisions had to be made prior to drawing the blueprints for construction. Those early interviews of business and industry leaders had revealed a need for welding and automobile mechanics. Neither program was appropriate for a downtown high-rise such as El Centro. To respond to the business communities needs as soon as possible, the two programs were placed at the next two campuses. Eastfield offered the auto mechanics program, as well as auto body repair, and Mountain View offered welding. The opening of each college was a success. That fall, the combined enrollments of El Centro, Mountain View, and Eastfield was 13,573 in credit classes and an additional six-thousand in non credit classes.[18]

The need was apparent for the fourth campus. Plans were being implemented for Richland College with a targeted opening date of fall 1972. Richland was located on 243 acres on the outer perimeter of Dallas at the southern edge of Richardson, a small suburban town in far north Dallas County. Richardson Independent School District had already considered opening a junior college so the opening of the newest college of the Dallas Junior College system was highly anticipated. Again the parking lot encircled the college buildings; however, most were built more similarly to the university model of a collection of stand alone buildings. This return to an older style campus layout was motivated by the aesthetic goal of taking advantage of the natural landscape. A bridge connects the two sections of the campus that are split by an elongated pond. This simple approach to capitalizing on the terrain precipitated many elements that became part of the culture of the campus. The employee newsletter is titled *The Bridge* and the ducks that inhabited the pond inspired the mascot, Thunder Ducks.[19] When Richland's doors opened to its first students in the fall of 1972, the district enrollment soared. The number rose again when, a month later, the first students enrolled in telecourses offered by the Dallas district.[20]

It was far from the first college to use television as a vehicle for delivery of credit classes, but the Dallas district quickly became one of the best. Educational television programs were part of the early experiments of broadcasting as early as 1933 when the medium itself was an evolving experiment. In the early fifties, Southern Methodist University televised a credit course on KRLD, the CBS affiliate at the time, but it was short lived. About the same time that Dallas was developing televised courses, Miami Dade in Florida built a full production center, however, after a couple of years it had produced only one course.[21]

When Priest first experimented with instructional television in Sacramento he learned what components were problematic and what production was needed to make it successful. One of the hindrances was lack of funding. Dallas had the budget to support the venture.[22] Even with an adequate budget, seeding the teleccourse project with one-half to one million dollars of risk capital took courage. Priest never shied from taking risks and encouraged responsible risk-taking from everyone who worked for him. Motivation for taking the risk, outside the basic goal of innovative approaches to delivering education and reaching new students, were the facts that the demand for classes was out pacing what could be offered on the existing campuses, and telecourses would reach currently un-served students.[23]

Priest had fought the reimbursement battle with the state of California. The state thought reimbursement for students who never came to campus was unethical. Priest thought Texas was fertile ground for taking education to the airwaves and well worth the tussles with the educational governing bodies of the state. The DCCCD board liked and supported the idea. On September 11, 1972, the first Dallas district telecourse, Government 201, was broadcast over KERA, Channel 13, the public broadcast affiliate in the Dallas-Fort Worth area.[24]

The role of supervising instructional television was part of the duties of the assistant to the chancellor. The first director of instructional television in that combined position was Travis Linn, former director at television station WFAA, the ABC affiliate in Dallas. He brought the knowledge of the broadcast industry and moved the program forward until he resigned in 1976. Linn had a background more appropriate for Instructional Television than the educational aspect of assistant to a college district chancellor. Placing such an important and innovative aspect of instruction under the supervision of anyone other than the academic vice-chancellor seemed perhaps inappropriate. Priest had the function report directly to him to protect it. According to Priest, as a direct report to him, it was less likely to "suffer the pot shots from critics who would kill it prematurely."[25] His plan was that once it was solidly established as a credible means of instruction, he would move it to the vice-chancellor, who at that time was R. Jan LeCroy, for further development and growth.

Indeed, telecourses had critics, most specifically faculty who were fearful of loss of academic integrity. The concern was genuine, and in keeping with the Priest's own desire for quality in every aspect of the district, two separate studies were conducted on two separate telecourses: a business course and a writing course. The findings in each set of data indicated higher performance and achievement by the telecourse students than the classroom students.[26]

From the first course produced in the Learning Resource Center at Richland College in 1972, the telecourse division quickly grew to a staff of seven by 1974. In 1975, it moved to portable buildings. By 1976, with eleven courses having been completed and others in production, the Instructional Television Division (ITV) was one of the country's two major producers of quality television courses and the division was under the supervision of the academic vice-chancellor.[27]

The year of 1972 was momentous for the Dallas County Junior College District. Richland College opened, the first telecourse was broadcast, and an additional eighty-five million dollars in bonds were sold. Also, earlier that year, the district officially changed its name to Dallas County Community College District. Every component of the Dallas district reflected the community college mission, except the name. While Priest and the board were on the cutting edge in facilities, curriculum, and services, they did not lead the way with the name change.

In the early fifties Jesse Bogue, the executive secretary of the American Association of Junior Colleges from 1946 to 1958, wrote a landmark book called *The Community College.* "Community" was added to the name of the association making it the American Association of Community and Junior Colleges during the tenure of Bogue's successor, Ed Gleazer. When Gleazer took the helm of the association, the position was changed to executive director and later president. Gleazer wrote extensively about the broader mission of the community college beyond offering post-secondary education. The use of the term community college began to spread. In 1963, the state of Florida, while keeping the two-year colleges part of the public school system, began using the term "community junior college."[28] Priest never preferred the use of the word "junior" as a descriptor of the two-year college, but it was historically associated and changing it would take more than his opinion.

The philosophy that led the Dallas Board of Trustees to establish a multi-college district was the catalyst that led to the name change which occurred by unanimous vote in January, 1972. Priest was using the term "community college" in 1962 with an expectation that two-year colleges should operate as an integral part of the community their colleges served. This brought a responsibility of providing entertainment and cultural events in addition to an array of courses.[29]

In Dallas, Priest had established all of the elements that distinguished the comprehensive community college from the junior college. The focus was on providing a multiplicity of services and supports for a student body diverse in ethnicity, age, and preparedness, to make them successful in whatever educational endeavor they pursued. Priest and the Board of Trustees realized that whether a student completed academic core courses for transfer to a university, a technical/vocational associate degree, or a non credit course to up-date skills, that education would make them marketable in the workplace. The ultimate outcome would be economic growth for the area with improved quality of life for its residents. The district served all of Dallas County, but it did so through its individual colleges. Each college served a distinct community with specific needs. The name change gave the district a verbal visage of commitment to all the people of Dallas County.[30]

The reputation of the Dallas County Community College District was already one of a national model. Just as in its beginning Priest and the board members took tours of the most innovative two-year colleges of the time, the DCCCD colleges were now the destination points of tours by many new and growing colleges. In 1974, Dale Parnell, chancellor of San Diego Community College District, brought the Board of Trustees to look at the Dallas system. The San Diego district had opened in 1969, and Parnell and his board came to gather ideas from the DCCCD. A main goal was to study and implement the DCCCD governance model. It was a compliment to Priest and the DCCCD Board of Trustees to have the chancellor and board of a large metropolitan community college district view them and their district as the model. Parnell was a man who knew and understood the comprehensive community college's relevance to the higher education system in the United States. He was selected to succeed Gleazer as president of the American Association of Community and Junior Colleges when Gleazer retired in 1981. Under Parnell's leadership, the word "junior" was dropped from the association's name to reflect the growing national trend. Priest had anticipated that community colleges were the wave of the future and the wave was at high tide.[31]

The DCCCD had two more colleges ready to begin construction and one more on the drawing board. Although the building schedule was an ambitious one, it did not keep pace with student numbers. By 1975, the combined credit enrollment of El Centro, Mountain View, Eastfield, Richland, and telecourses was thirty-four-thousand.[32] The following year, the district had projected and budgeted for a five percent increase in enrollment. They received a nineteen percent increase bringing the total to over forty-thousand. That would have been even more, but they were forced to run public service announcements on the radio and send press releases to the newspapers stating that the campuses were full. Approximately three-thousand students were turned away.[33]

Having to turn away three-thousand students might be termed a "good problem," but it was unacceptable to Priest. This was doubly painful for Priest because he and the board had anticipated the need for additional space and planned to raze a portion of the structure housing El Centro to construct a new facility that would increase the usable square footage. The Sanger Brother's building was actually a composite of two buildings constructed at separate times. The district's plan was placed on hold while they battled with the Dallas Historic Preservation League and the Texas Antiquities Commission over the historical value of the Sanger Brothers' buildings. These two organizations wanted to preserve the buildings.[34] Architects lined up on both sides. Expert opinions were mixed on the feasibility of restoration to salvage the buildings versus razing them and constructing new buildings. The DCCCD had conducted a study that revealed the buildings, while externally representative of the nineteenth century business architecture, had been quickly and cheaply constructed, not intended for long term use. On personal inspection, Priest found there were parts of the building where the stone flaked off in his hand. The eighteen-month brouhaha went all the way to the Texas Supreme Court and cost the district 1.9 million dollars in unused construction contracts and litigation.[35] The loss was so high because the two historic preservation groups had not been timely in their protests and contracts had already been negotiated and signed for the demolition of the old buildings and construction of the new structure.[36]

The end result was the salvaging of the external shell of the nine-story building. Eight stories had been built in 1884. The ninth floor had been added by the DCCCD to house district offices. The original structure was and is an example of the Richardsonian architectural influence and by all counts the most historically significant of the three separately constructed phases of the facility.[37] Even though the district had ample resources, the loss of nearly two million dollars was significant, and in hindsight, there was a question of whether or not partial victory was worth the loss in time and money. Analysis of the evidence does not provide a clear answer. Steve Mittlestet was working as Priest's assistant at that time. In an interview in 1994, he reflected, "While it is good to be part of preserving some of the history of downtown Dallas, because there is so little of that, the building has never been at the level it needed to be to serve the students of El Centro."[38]

Linda Timmerman was Priest's secretary in 1976. In an interview in 2002, she remembered that she had never seen Priest as angry and frustrated as he was during that litigious process. It is still a sore spot with him. The solution would have been for the district to have acted faster and to have had the building razed before the Dallas Historic Preservation League and the Texas Antiquities Commission could have intervened with legal action. At the end of the legal proceedings, all of the construction contracts had to be renegotiated. The cost of construction materials had escalated.[39]

Years of use by frustrated students and faculty proved Priest to be right, that the structure was inadequate for the growing needs of the college and was functionally inadequate. Modern additions have been added next to the old Sanger Brothers' building. The historical building's shell remains intact, but the internal structure has been renovated many times. When El Centro first opened, long time residents and patrons of Sanger Brothers Department Store could easily visualize where the jewelry counter had been or where the notions department used to be. Now it takes viewing the building from afar to recall its department store days. Inside, it is clearly a community college, designed to serve students.

For all the rancor of that year-and-a-half struggle, 1976 was not without its positives. That year, Priest was named to the Athletic Hall of Fame in Stockton, California. It gave him the opportunity to travel back to the place of his childhood and see old friends. The following year, Priest received one of the highest honors of his career. The American Association of College Baseball Coaches inducted him into the Hall of Fame for former baseball players who rise to the top of their chosen career field. The plaque reads, "Bill Priest whose career achievement reflects the ideals that sports exemplify."[40] This recognition carried with it double significance. It validated his baseball career and credited him with moving beyond to greater success. After all, it could be said that he hit a grand slam in higher education.

Not every decision made by Priest and the DCCCD board was met with full acceptance by faculty and staff. In 1976, a decision for an organizational change was made based on practicality. The division chair position was a nine-month faculty position, which meant there was no one in that office during the summer unless the chair was given a summer contract at formula pay, meaning a percentage of the nine-month salary. Logic indicated the job was clearly a twelve-month job and one annual administrative contract cost less than a nine-month faculty contract plus one or two summer contracts. This change created a controversy among district employees, especially faculty. Those faculty members in the chair positions were given a choice of changing to administration or returning to teaching. Most saw it as a pay cut and demotion, and chose to return to teaching. Other faculty members believed it diminished faculty voice in governance because a faculty division chair was more able to support faculty and instruction than an administrator in that role. Stan Fulton, an instructor at Mountain View College, disagreed with Priest's decision but supported him as a leader. He recalled, "Unfortunately, the faculty in those division chair jobs became a little too greedy and kept demanding more money and extra service contracts, and so, like the consummate autocrat, he was not satisfied with simply telling them no. He had to kick their collective ass with this solution."[41] Fulton went on to explain that Priest was not a liar and that the faculty always knew the real reasons behind decisions. That elicits respect even if not agreement. Fulton summed up his opinion by describing Priest as "a tough, smart, brutally honest, fair and upfront old bastard, community college god that I respect immensely."[42]

North Lake and Cedar Valley were scheduled to open in the fall of the following year and that decision had repercussions in some of the early staffing decisions. Outside applicants complained about a closed system which was more perception than reality. As the district opened new campuses, current employees were given opportunities to transfer to the new campuses, sometimes in their current position and sometimes into a new career opportunity. That left openings at the old campuses and there were plenty of new positions remaining open at the new campuses. It allowed many opportunities for advancement within the district while still providing ample openings for the many educational professionals interested in joining the ranks of a highly respected college district.[43]

A line drawn from the proposed Cedar Valley campus and the North Lake campus cut diagonally across Dallas County, and it was the same with Eastfield and Mountain View, which opened simultaneously seven years earlier. Cedar Valley was built on 353 acres in a rural section of Lancaster in south Dallas County. The main buildings nestle around a two-level, landscaped stone courtyard. The whole campus backs on to a large pond. In keeping with selecting curriculum for each college that responded to community and business needs, an additional auto mechanics program was placed at Cedar Valley. The surrounding small towns were rooted in a history of farms and ranches leading to the establishment of a veterinary technician program there. The facilities are a distance from the main campus. They include a full veterinary clinic and housing for both large and small animals with a corral for horses and cattle. The area was not heavily populated at the time, but this college district was being built for the future. Since there was a large pond (or very small lake, depending on who was giving the description) on one side of the campus, parking was restricted to the other side with a road and a circular drive separating it from the main campus. The gymnasium was built as a separate building on the southwest side of the campus with parking on the west side of that building. It was not as commuter friendly as the previous campus layouts. It was, however, like all of the campuses, beautiful. The future that had been planned for arrived in the late eighties with the creation of Joe Pool Lake and new housing developments in nearby Cedar Hill and DeSoto.

North Lake College was built on 276 acres in Irving on the west side of Dallas County. The multi-leveled buildings flowed like a single structure and were staggered along the side of a hill. Parking was placed on two sides of the campus. One lot sits at the top of the hill at the main street entrance with a long downhill hike to the buildings. The other lot rests in a small valley with a long hike up to the buildings. The campus proper was built with covered walkways and halls connecting most of the buildings with stairs and ramps. The structure from the backside is reminiscent of an ancient Mayan dwelling.

There was a true focus on architectural solutions to educational concerns and a desire that form and structure represent the intended function. North Lake, and later Brookhaven, was built with open laboratories and spaces to facilitate self-paced learning. This new instructional approach was supported by flex-entry scheduling and fast-tracked courses.[44] The concept was new and not sufficiently tested, but Priest's dedication to innovation was paramount above tried and true comfortable methods. He believed that if one was not making mistakes, they were not trying enough new things.[45]

Cedar Valley and North Lake both opened in the summer of 1977. The following year, the final Dallas County Community College opened in Farmers Branch in far northeast Dallas County. Like North Lake, Brookhaven was built with open spaces for self-paced instruction. An additional auto mechanics program was established at Brookhaven, and that campus was to offer nursing courses in conjunction with El Centro. By the mid-seventies, the number of working mothers had created a surge in the child care business. A program in child development was set-up at Brookhaven with a stand alone fully operational Child Development Center complete with a fenced-in play area. The center was to be used as a lab school for Brookhaven students and was open to the public. The same program had been established at Eastfield and both programs garnered such excellent reputations among the parents in each community that waiting lists were soon necessary for enrollment. The warning to young women who worked in the district was as soon as they knew they were pregnant, they needed to get on the waiting list. The quality of the child care there continues, causing the length of the waiting lists to grow at both colleges.[46]

Another similarity Brookhaven had to North Lake, was the multi-levels built along the rolling terrain. The buildings are separated by several natural courtyards with trees, foliage, and fountains. The roofs angled to a pitch on one side of each building and were covered in copper and were quite visible from the nearby freeway. Another very visible structure on the Brookhaven campus was to be the one-hundred-and-twenty-foot tall windmill in the center courtyard. This was the last and greatest attempt at blending practicality, art and image marketing. In an article in the *Dallas Morning News* in December of 1976 announcing the plans for the mega-structure, Priest was quoted, "If we pull this thing off, it will certainly be an attraction."[47] At that time, Priest did not realize the size of that "if."

The design of the windmill was a center pole suspended twelve feet from the ground by steel pipes and cables crisscrossed to give the illusion of suspension in space. It was to have eight blades and be fully operational. The primary reason for building a windmill on a college campus was to give Brookhaven College a symbol that linked the future and the past. The past was the agrarian heritage of Farmers Branch.[48] The idea came from the architectural firm of Pratt, Box, and Henderson.[49] An afterthought was the practical application of the windmill to provide water to the shower facilities serving the gym and to power the fountains in the courtyards.[50] It was thought there was even potential use by physics students for experimentation. The design was based on a smaller German model.[51]

Priest recalled that the construction of the windmill was a bold move and at the time its size or artistic value were not questioned. The main risk was justification of the projected cost of $170,000, which was three-fourths of one percent of the total construction cost of the campus.[52] As problems began to arise in the construction of the windmill, so did the cost. First, the engineers disagreed about the soundness of replicating a thirty-foot piece of art into a 120 foot functional windmill. Then came the sequential calamities that befell the blades which had been made in Germany, shipped to the United States, and then trucked to Dallas. The first set of blades was lost when the truck transporting them from Houston had a wreck. Some months later, when the truck carrying the second set of blades arrived safely and the doors to the truck were opened, the blades had been damaged in transport. The bands used to secure the blades during the long trip had cut into the resin-like material and left multiple gouges along the edges of each blade. At that point, everyone felt it was time to quit and find an alternative.[53]

Some quasi blades were put in place, but when they turned, the vibration posed safety concerns. Those blades were removed.[54]

When Patsy Fulton came to Brookhaven College as the new president in 1984, the first thing waiting for her attention was a letter from the mayor of Farmers Branch. The letter explained that special permission had been given to the district to erect the windmill because it exceeded he city's height restrictions. That permission was predicated on the promise that the windmill would be a working generator. The main point of the letter according to Fulton was "to get it working or get it down."[55]

In researching the issue, Fulton could not find an engineering firm that would declare the windmill safe or capable of generating any significant amount of electricity. Fulton notified the chancellor, R. Jan LeCroy, who told her it was her decision. Fulton then began the process for removal of the windmill. The campus community expressed mixed feelings. Some were glad to see the intimidating structure go, and others protested the removal of a piece of art. The engineering firm that disassembled it warned that it was spring-loaded and they were unsure of what might occur in taking it down. The deconstruction was scheduled for spring break of 1985 and took place without incident.[56] Fulton recalled that just a few weeks after the removal, she was walking behind several older women who seemed to be touring the campus. She heard one talking about the massive piece of art that was in one of the courtyards and surely they would find it if they just kept walking. Fulton said she momentarily felt a flush of guilt.

The Brookhaven College windmill, in retrospect, was a mistake with an unknown total cost to the district. It was as though no one wanted to add up the actual expenditures associated with the windmill project from concept to removal.[57] In the planning stages, engineers and architects had advised it was an exciting and history making undertaking. Based on the recommendations of the architects, Priest secured the approval of the board.[58]

The structure was still in place at the time of Priest's retirement. A windmill is still used as the Brookhaven logo and is part of the campus culture. Everyone who worked at Brookhaven anytime between 1978 and 1985 seems to have a windmill story. The windmill will always be part of the college's legends and myths. Memories often embellish a good story.

In 1978, with the last college opened, the growth and innovation did not stop. Enrollments in telecourses had grown to over ten-thousand per academic year. Eighteen courses had been produced and were being sought after by other colleges and even business and industry. That year, Roger Pool became the first telecourse supervisor to have instructional television as his sole responsibility, and he reported to the vice-chancellor of academic affairs, R. Jan LeCroy. That same year a district-wide task force recommended changing the name of Instructional Television to the Center for Telecommunications. Priest's speculation that there was much value in pre-produced quality courses televised for student convenience had proven to be right on the mark.[59]

He was also right on the mark in his support of marketing as an essential element of a successful college district. Among some gasps and clucking of tongues over wasted time and money, Priest approved and funded a marketing workshop for all the district's administrators. It was organized by the District Public Information Office. At the event, then national marketing expert Phil Kotler and his colleagues Dennis Johnson and Ernie Leach talked about academic programs in terms of "cash cows" and "dead dogs." They explained that one component of program evaluation needed to be profitability. They told the somewhat skeptical audience that colleges needed to do statistical research to determine which academic programs were drawing students and which were not. The statistical approach of the second part of the analysis began to convince some of its validity. The analysis would include a viability study of the program to judge whether increased marketing would help to increase enrollment or whether the program should be phased out. The District Public Information Director, Claudia Robinson, said that her counterparts in community colleges across the country were astounded that Priest would take such a bold step. Most college presidents and chancellors were reluctant to even buy advertising.[60]

The Dallas County Community College District was the first in the country to have an insert in the prominent high school magazine, *Campus Voice*. Even Priest was reluctant at first, but he always was willing to listen and consider good data. With the presentation of additional facts, Priest gave his support for the insert which proved to be profitable.[61]

Robinson described Priest as "masterful, intelligent, visionary, and sustaining"[62] in his utilization of marketing. He was always ready to take the risk of being first. In 1978, he hired Peat, Marwick, and Mitchell to conduct a marketing audit of what the district was doing and should be doing. That audit recommended an image and awareness survey of the DCCCD's service area. Priest then hired MARC, a research company, to conduct that survey in 1979. Based on those results the public information staff created the 1980 advertising campaign, "Real Colleges. Real Careers. Really close to home." The survey had revealed a prevailing public opinion that community colleges were not colleges, but a bridge between high school and college. The campaign aimed to confront the perception head on in order to change it.[63]

Again in 1978, the DCCCD's seven colleges were the first community colleges to use a mixed media campaign that tied print advertising to radio commercials. At that time, other colleges were relying on public service announcements and a few were running newspaper advertisements.[64] Public service announcements were free, but were aired at times chosen by the radio station and vied for time with more notable causes like medical research fund raising. That same year the DCCCD hosted the regional National Council for Community Relations Conference, but only twelve public information professionals attended.[65] That was a numerical representation of the lack of value placed on that function by most community colleges. With the DCCCD leading the way, by 1981 well over fifty public information officers from Texas colleges attended the regional conference.[66]

Priest appreciated the value of marketing and the power of the media whether that information was an unsolicited article or a paid advertisement. The only negative experience he had with the Dallas media was with *D Magazine*. In 1980, Bill Bancroft conducted a thorough review of the district with multiple interviews. Most had a sense he was looking for "dirt."[67] The article took the tone of investigative reporting. But there was nothing scathing. The worst Bancroft could find were the early days of private board meetings before the public official meetings. There were a few people who complained that Priest was not a proponent of participatory management, but there were more who praised Priest for his open, honest, and fair approach to management. The article also cited a 1980 Southern Associaiton of Colleges and Schools accreditation team who criticized the district for having too many faculty who had earned their degrees from Texas Colleges. Approximately eighty to eighty-five percent of the faculty had degrees from Texas colleges. The article also criticized the DCCCD for lacking in diversity among its administrators and faculty members.[68] At that time, there were several African-Americans and Latinos working as college and district level administrators and there were two female college presidents, one of whom was African-American. The criticisms were true and noted, but neither had escalated into an internal or external controversy; nor were they unique to the DCCCD. These were issues common to growing community colleges in metropolitan areas in the late 1970s and early 1980s.[69]

In order to gather adequate information for the article, Bancroft spent several weeks in the district interviewing people. According to Priest, Bancroft dogged him relentlessly. A couple of days after the magazine issue with the DCCCD article hit the stands, Priest went to a Cowboys football game to relax. It was the beginning of the first quarter when Priest spotted Bancroft in the stands with ticket in hand searching for his seat. Bancroft looked at the rows carefully as he came closer and closer to Priest. Like an inescapable Moirai, Bancroft located his seat; the number placed him right beside Priest. Priest said it almost ruined the game.[70]

CHAPTER SEVEN

Bill Jason Priest

The Man Personally and Professionally

In a *Dallas Morning News* article in 1995, the description was given, "He was a thoroughly upright, cantankerous, feisty individual, and Americans have always had a soft spot for that type of figure."[1] Those were the words of a political science professor from Tulane University about Harry S. Truman. It could have been said of Bill J. Priest. It was not, however, sentimentality that has caused history to view Truman as a political icon or Priest as a community college icon. It is the strength of character of each. Each man led with a forthrightness with no hidden agendas, no phoniness, just plain "what you see is what you get." Both men also represented the common man, unpretentious, and without guile.

The man Priest is personally is the man he was professionally. In personal interviews and written descriptions, the first word on the list of adjectives describing Priest was honest or truthful. This was followed by such phrases as "straight shooter," "no false signals," and the certainty of knowing where he stood and where you stood in his estimation. This was consistent with personal friends, professional acquaintances, and his detractors. Priest always diminished compliments of any kind with a deflecting bit of humor.

He often said, "I don't have a good enough memory to lie." The consensus is that truthfulness is what he values in others and demands of himself. Diogenes, the Greek Cynic philosopher in the mid-first century who carried a lantern about in the daylight in search of an honest man, could have ceased searching if he had met Bill Priest.

Complete honesty is a double-edged sword. Most people are not prepared to handle total honesty especially if it is wielded toward them. Priest did not use tact and finesse in his straightforward presentation of criticisms and direct enumeration of mistakes. This bluntness was not well received by some. Betty Meachum, psychology instructor at Cedar Valley College, remembered feeling humiliated in front of her peers in her first encounter with Priest. She was the newly elected faculty association president from her campus and in the initial district council meeting, all seven of the outgoing presidents, the seven new incoming presidents, and the vice chancellors were present. They were having a discussion about sabbatical approval notifications for faculty. Quite often the faculty member was being congratulated by colleagues before receiving official notification. The discussion concluded with Priest adding to the minutes that the first part of the notification process would be a "rah rah letter" sent from his office. Meachum recalled, "I sort of laughed and said, 'I can tell you really mean that.' The room fell deathly silent. He looked at me and said, 'I do mean it, and if you knew me better, you'd know that I mean it. I hope you get to know me well enough to know that I mean it.' I think he was insensitive about how his direct manner could hurt people."[2]

Priest did mean it. He cared about all the employees. He respected faculty and wanted them to feel appreciated and honored. His seemingly sarcastic description of the letter was his laconic style. If a bit of slang could convey his message, that's what he used. He was being to the point that the concern about notification had been heard and would be addressed. He did not use unnecessary flowery accolades or a long line of adjectives, considering them to be superfluous.

Although his attitude was sometimes difficult to take, almost everyone indicated it was easier to do what was expected when it was made clear as to what those expectations were. You did not have to be fearful of unspoken motivations or attempts at manipulation. Reba Blackshear, president of the DCCCD Faculty Association Council in 1980, respected Priest's no frills honesty. She indicated that it translated into fairness when negotiating with faculty. She said, "I tell him exactly what I think . . . I respect a person I disagree with, and he is fair every time."[3]

One newspaper account in California in 1960 reported a faculty member saying, "Priest wants what is best for Priest, and woe to anyone who gets in his way." The article described the feelings among the employees at American River College as ranging from "real dislike to near hero worship."[4] By all accounts, that range persisted in Dallas as well. *D Magazine* quoted a faculty member who presented himself as the spokesperson for the whole faculty, "The faculty are kind of intimidated. They know their place. . . . If you're good, you get to go to work in the big house. If not, you got to go work in their field, and it's hot out there."[5]

Obviously Priest did not enjoy ubiquitous admiration. Even his most severe critics, however, acquiesced to the evidence of his accomplishments. One DCCCD administrator, who asked for anonymity, expressed contempt for Priest and described him as controlling and brutally honest in expressing his opinion about people. That same person expressed respect for Priest professionally and admiration for the things he had accomplished in and for higher education. The criticisms of Priest generally were that he wielded power in order to control, or that he blatantly presented his opinion as fact, or used his verbal adroitness to skewer unsuspecting victims.

Of those who could be categorized as "hero worshipers," Priest's shortcomings seemed to be dismissed or viewed as positives. The first president of the first faculty association in the district, Gayle Weaver said, "There was no question of who was captain of the ship, but he acknowledged the value of the faculty and always took suggestions. He was the best man for the job. I never saw weaknesses."

A weakness, like beauty, is in the eye of the beholder. His attempt to control was sometimes an unintended influence. Betty Meachum was elected Cedar Valley Faculty Association president a second time. She recalled an incident where a biased critical remark from Priest probably cost an instructor his sabbatical. The faculty association presidents from each of the seven colleges had gathered to review faculty applications for sabbaticals. The group was charged with selecting five to recommend to the Board of Trustees. For convenience and privacy they were meeting downtown in Priest's office. A couple of times Priest came through to get something from his desk or file. On the second time through his office, Priest asked how it was coming. They had narrowed the list to around ten and read those names to Priest. According to Meachum, at the reading of one instructor's name, Priest cavalierly said as he was walking out, "You mean you'd give a sabbatical to that long-haired hippie?"[7] Meachum felt the remark was unprofessional, and it was not discussed in anyway, no one in the group even referred to it. But, in the final decision, the instructor did not get a sabbatical. Meachum believed the group had been swayed by that passing remark, not from fear of retribution from Priest, but because he was so deeply respected that his opinion was powerfully influential.

Priest described himself as blunt, but not capricious. He said he decided early in his life that truthfulness was easier because it was all too complicated to mislead. Although unbridled honesty can sting, he did not shield himself from the returning shots. He believed it was the job of the chief administrator to protect the institution by remaining in the line of fire. It was the duty of the president or chancellor to step up to meet the challenge, whatever it was, and to take the criticism, from whomever it came. In his own words in an article published in the *Junior College Journal* in 1962, he defined the lead role of an institution of higher education as meaning, "You are obliged and privileged to be the prime target."[8] He also stated that the best defense is being armed with accurate information.

Priest's personal values of honesty, monogamous relationships, traditional lifestyles, unquestionable integrity, a strong work ethic, punctuality, and obedience to the laws of the land influenced his professional decisions. He never imposed his values on others. There were times people would bring him stories about behaviors of DCCCD employees outside of their jobs. Priest ignored these. His only concern was its affect on job performance or possible harm from negative opinions in the community.

Some disagreed with his decisions. Some disagreed with his values. Abiding by the guide that kept his view of personal lives and professional performance separate, the integrity of the district was never brought into question. According to the District Public Information Office staff, on three different occasions *D Magazine* sent reporters to scour the files and interview employees looking for a bit of scandalous activity to report. Only one of the investigations resulted in an article with a few true, but unremarkable, criticisms. In fact, that same article quoted Trustee Robert Powell about conducting his own investigation. Powell said, "I spent many, many hours poring over past budgets, and past studies, and past everything. I finally became convinced we had a very good college district."[9]

That same year, Jerry Gilmore was board chair and he said of Priest, "He has undergone the most exacting scrutiny of media and assorted critics, and he has never been found wanting."[10] Bob Thornton, the founding board chair, never denied that Priest's decisions were not always popular, but pointed to the fact people respected Priest for playing fair, being honest, and making decisions impartially based on what was best for the colleges and the students.

Someone who knew Priest very well and from many perspectives was Deon Holt. He had been a faculty member under Priest's leadership in California and later he worked with him in Dallas. Holt had served as the vice chancellor of planning and development, president of Richland College, and president of Brookhaven College. In describing Priest's management style, he referred to a book he had read in the mid-seventies on leadership, *The Gamesman* by Michael Maccoby. He felt Priest fit the profile presented in the book as "the jungle fighter." Maccoby described this leader as an entrepreneur, empire builder, pragmatically progressive, with leanings toward being a social Darwinist. The jungle fighter is one who promotes new technology and keeps the tribe (organization) moving forward, but sometimes at the expense of people's feelings. This type of leader has the ability to sway people's opinions and dominates through superior ideas, courage, and strength. He rewards loyalty, and his followers both fear and revere him.[11] The description of the jungle fighter depicts a leader who succeeds with forward moving accomplishments and engenders emotional extremes in those he leads, a description which closely parallels some other's perceptions of Priest.

Going deeper than just a judgment of whether it was good or bad, there were varied interpretations about Priest's leadership and management style. Some even thought it was paternalistic. An example given was Priest's policy that faculty members be allowed to teach only one semester in the summer. The reason he gave, recalled accounting instructor Clarice McCoy, was that every faculty member needed at least one summer semester off to rest because teaching was such a demanding job. Demonstrative of the duality of perceptions, she added, "It was such a condescending policy. He was so paternal. But he was the best [chancellor] we ever had. Those were the glory days."[12]

Whether it might be the halo factor in memories or not, the "glory days" is a phrase frequently used by early employees in describing the first twelve years of the DCCCD. Founding president of El Centro, Don Rippey, titled his book about those beginning years, *Some Called it Camelot.*

Claudia Robinson did not join the DCCCD staff until 1976 when she was hired as the district director of public information. She came from the corporate world of public relations. She lists Priest as the best supervisor she ever had. She, too, equates his leadership style with the somewhat controversial style of Harry S. Truman. She described Priest as having the courage of his convictions, and realizing that the buck stopped with him because if it didn't stop somewhere, there would be chaos. She said he hired good people and then let them do their jobs. Robinson also confirmed his confrontational nature. She said, "If someone really made a blunder, he let you know about it immediately and would often verbally go for the jugular vein, but then you would never hear about it again. You always knew where you stood with Dr. Priest. You might not like it, but you were always sure."[13]

The similarities of Priest and Truman are numerous and were noted by several additional people. The very qualities that brought each of them criticism are the same ones which garnered appreciation and admiration. While President of the American Association of Community and Junior Colleges, Dale Parnell gave Priest a photo of Priest delivering a speech at the AACJC conference and signed it "Give 'Em Hell, Harry."[14]

In response to that frequent campaign cheer, Truman once said, "I never gave anybody hell. I just told the truth and they thought it was hell."[15] That was the prevailing opinion among those who were close to Priest. They felt he never gave anyone hell, that those who had been admonished or strongly criticized by Priest had been told only what was accurate and true.

Both men have been described as having a clear vision of what their responsibilities were in their respective roles. Truman understood what it meant to lead a nation, but had the qualities of the common man. Priest, too, understood people from every walk of life. He could discuss government issues with officials at the state and national levels and he could discuss the skills needed to get a good job with a high school drop-out. The district was a growing success in 1971 when a reporter for the *Dallas Morning News* attributed Priest's part in that success to being in touch with the common man, and not being a blue sky academician, nor educational elitist.[16]

Truman also was lauded for his ability to act decisively and swiftly. Priest, too, was called decisive and a man of action. Rudolph Giuliani, the mayor of New York City during the 9-11 terrorist attack, in his book, *Leadership*, gives quick decision making as a necessary attribute for leadership. He explained there must be a balance between speed and deliberation and the key is in knowing how to act when there's not much time to deliberate.[17] Educators place a high value on the process of decision making. The nature of the situation does not always allow for forming a committee to gather data, evaluate and discuss, and time to build a consensus of the college community. For example, if the state legislature sends out an edict with the expectation that all public institutions of higher learning will comply, that can require immediate action. Actions taken by the district administration without campus input can be viewed as dictatorial or non-participatory decision making at best.

Don Rippey said unequivocally that Priest was an autocratic leader but he qualified that label by saying it was the acceptable style of the times. He further described typical leadership of the sixties as prescriptive and directive and that Priest was very good at using those characteristics. He also credited Priest with caring about people which tempered his direct control methods.[18]

Priest was keenly aware of the perceptions that he was an autocratic leader. When asked about this opinion held by many of the employees in the DCCCD, without hesitation, he boldly answered, "I cultivated that perception." He explained that by the nature of his job, he was ultimately responsible for what transpired in the district and ethical controls were essential. Whatever prescriptive action was deemed necessary by the situation was easier to affect if everyone already had the impression of the chancellor as being an authoritarian figure. Priest said, "No one is surprised if I issue a directive if they believe me to be autocratic. They just say, 'What'd you expect,' and they do it." Always the pragmatist even at the expense of his own self-image, Priest put the well being of the district above all else.[19]

Priest did not want anyone trying to explain or excuse his behavior when it was criticized. He calls himself blunt and stubborn to a fault, but prefers that people confront him with their disagreement rather than discuss it with colleagues. His secretary in the late seventies, Linda Timmerman, said she had once tried to explain to an unhappy employee what was behind a decision that Priest had made. She told Priest about it, and he admonished her. He told her not to offer explanations for which she may not have all the facts. He said he did not need her to defend him but to advise the person to come to him and express their concerns. Timmerman said she realized that he was right.[20]

Priest was confident and self assured, but did not approach management with an unbending attitude. Some thought so, but those who worked closely with him knew he would listen to facts. Priest was a believer in researching a matter thoroughly before taking it to a group for discussion. In an article written for new college presidents, Priest warned them not to pretend to know all the answers because no one knows all the answers. He mused, "Don't let it be said of you, 'He may be wrong, but he is never in doubt."[21] Mittlestet, Holt, Robinson, and numerous others have given accounts of bringing in new ideas, or disagreeing with decisions that had been made, and that after a presentation of additional information, Priest had changed his mind. Robinson added, "But you better have your ducks all in a row and be prepared to answer good probing questions."[22]

Perhaps the best summation of Priest's strong but sometimes controversial leadership style came form a reporter with the *Sacramento Union* newspaper in an article announcing Priest's appointment as the first superintendent of Los Rios Junior College District. His approval for the job had come on a split vote by the Los Rios Board of Trustees setting an uncertain tone for Priest's leadership. The reporter wrote, "Any man offering positive leadership must necessarily take a firm stand, which might not elicit universal approval from all, but this frequently is the price of such leadership. Priest is highly regarded as an able administrator among other junior college executives in the state."[23] With those words he ascribed personal integrity to Priest and presented decisiveness as an essential to good leadership.

At the top of the list of attributes needed for leadership is communication. Almost any book on leadership will delineate good communication as having verbal and writing skills, and knowing what to communicate and when. Priest did not consider himself to be a good public speaker. He felt that the more he prepared the worse his presentation was, but he did not feel that he was glib enough to rely on extemporaneous delivery. Those who have ever heard him give a speech disagree with his self-effacing estimation of his skills. His use of language is unique to him. His genuineness is apparent in his public presentations and his words and style do not vary when he is having an informal conversation. An important element of being an effective public speaker is the ability to read the audience. Priest has that skill as well as an understanding of what people want to hear and what they need to hear. When being introduced for a public address, Priest says that his part in Hiroshima and/or his baseball career are usually included in that introduction. The historic significance that Hiroshima holds gives a heroic aura to his persona and his stint in professional baseball adds interest to his profile as an educational professional. He uses the public's interest level in those subjects to the advantage of his main purpose. He explained, "I long ago found that when you are talking to lay groups about education, be sure you digress frequently into other topics because they are a hell of a lot more interested in those than they are in education. But you can sell a little education by currying their goodwill by talking about other things."[24] His philosophy is that nothing is worse than a dull drab speech regardless of the content. Priest believes it is the speaker's duty to be mercifully brief and to expand or exclude material based on the audience. Deny it though he might, Priest was and is an excellent and entertaining speaker. He reads his audiences well; he has marketing savvy and a natural wit, all attributes of good public speaking.

While not comfortable at the public podium during his professional career, he was completely comfortable in meetings or individual conversations with anyone from any background. His command of language and his breadth of knowledge made him an able conversationalist in any situation. In an article in *Scene Magazine* in 1971, Thornton said of Priest, "He can be talking finance one minute, approaching senators and congressmen about appropriations, and talk baseball or tennis the next. He can talk to and in the vernacular of every element we have [in Dallas]. To me, that is Bill's greatness. He is in every facet of education, but he is down to earth with his feet on the ground in everything from education to business."[25]

Priest's use of language intertwines the evidence of his level of education and years of voracious reading with the casualness of slang and colloquialisms, punctuated with the occasional expletive. He uses profanity with selectivity, however, and consideration of those in the room. The way he strings words together gives a freshness to familiar ideas and clarity to new ones. He can take a complex concept and reduce it to a concise statement. In a 1974 article on executive stress in *Sunday Magazine* in the *Dallas Times Herald,* Priest outlined what he labeled the "major dilemma of an executive career ladder." He said, "At what point are you as high as you should go—one step too high is tragic and yet you never know if you'll be good at the next level until you get there. But then it's almost impossible to turn back."[26] Although it was not his intention, Priest clearly stated in this succinct statement the essence of *The Peter Principle* by Laurence J. Peter.

Priest personally answered most of the communications sent to him. If it was a memo, he often wrote a response across the top or on a separate sheet of paper if it was a longer reply. He saw no reason to dictate to his secretary, have her type it, proof it, and perhaps retype it. He felt that would delay the response from him that would keep things moving. He knew what he wanted to say and how he wanted to say it. That was sufficient. Unlike many people in fast paced positions, his handwriting was as clear as his words. He did most of his work from his desk. This was not in an effort to avoid face to face encounters, quite the contrary. It was done because he wanted to be accessible by phone or available for appointment. There were no cell phones then and to be in the car was to be out of reach.

Priest's appreciation of the power of words caused him to give attention to their use and misuse. He knew when his position required him to respond. He was also well aware of when his expertise level on a subject might interfere with the best explanation. When Timmerman worked for him, she recalled hearing him tell the district lawyer his intent on a conference call they were going to have. According to Timmerman, Priest said, "Let me garble it for him for a time. Then I'll hang up and you straighten out what I just told him." Timmerman called the comment "classic Priest."[27]

Another form of expression that could be characterized as "classic Priest" was his amazingly successful use of slang. Just as it takes a very sophisticated and talented actor to perform physical comedy well, it was the cogency of Priest's speech that lent respectability to his use of slang. As a new chancellor in a newly forming college district, Priest used a subculture word that had been adopted by teenagers in talking about Dallas to a reporter from the *Dallas Morning News*. He was describing the attraction of the city with its reputation of being energetic and ambitious "with a feeling of destiny. This is real salable. People don't want to go to 'Dullsville,' but to a place that aspires to be topnotch, that will be professionally stimulating and rewarding."[28] He felt that if a word regarded as slang could make his point with fewer words, it was the better word. Some executives, just hired into one of the top positions in their field in a metropolitan area, might have viewed such casual use of language in the media as sounding unintelligent or an effort at sounding "hip" or youthful, but it was characteristic of Priest to be direct, concise, and casual. From him, it sounded intelligent and natural.

Just as natural to Priest was his use of humor, even at the most serious of moments. In an article he wrote in 1962, Priest warned new presidents that the position was a big job and that it was one requiring dignity, and that most achieved that level on ability and perseverance mixed with luck. Being overly impressed with one's position could result in becoming a dignified "stuffed shirt."[29] He was never hesitant to make himself the target of his own humor. On one of the most austere of occasions in his career, his formal request to the Dallas County Community College District Board of Trustees for his retirement, he made the point of this being the right time for him to retire with the use of humor. He referred to administrators who remained in the top leadership position longer than was appropriate as "old goats," and he added that he was sure there were those who thought he had long since joined their ranks.[30]

He never talked about his baseball career without zinging himself for his short duration in the major leagues. He called it the one career at which he was so "immensely unsuccessful." Since he had been a pitcher, he chided the batters in that they "were very uncooperative and ruined my career."[31]

A sense of humor, laconic speech with a proclivity for analysis, and his leadership positions in education brought Priest numerous speaking and writing requests. His lack of formal training in public address, something he felt was a negative, freed him to rely on his natural ability.

Priest's demeanor, like his speech, was a blend of appropriateness of etiquette and of one fully comfortable with informality, unmotivated by some inner need to impress. By the time he came to Dallas, his years behind the desk of community college leadership had added a few pounds to the muscular physique of his baseball and military years. His hair was beginning to thin and his choice of clothes, complete with bow tie, would not put him on the cover of *Gentleman's Quarterly*. At Priest's job interview these visual characteristics are what gave rise to the admonition of one DCCCD board member to another to simply listen to him and not to make judgments on his appearance. A similar observation was made by board chair Jerry Gilmore in 1980, when he told a reporter for *D Magazine*, "He is the kind of person that slips up on you. Sometimes he looks like he ought to be selling used cars. But if you listen to him, the man is incredibly intelligent, and he has a real grasp on the direction he feels he ought to go."[31] In various newspaper articles through the years, he had been described as "a big happy bear of a man,"[32] and as having "a superficial resemblance to heavyweight champion Ingemar Johansson."[33] More recent comparisons have been to the actor Rod Steiger. Some of the descriptions of his looks are influenced by the view of his sometimes pugnacious personality. While his words are strong, his voice is gentle. He has a warm smile and a glint in his eyes.

Priest is a happy man, meaning that he realizes happiness comes from within and not from external sources. Stress and frustrations are external. In a task as large and complex as opening and then running a multi-college district—with such varied constituencies, internal and external, to serve and keep happy—stress was inevitable. Priest understood the need for outlets for managing stress and for renewal. He enjoyed hunting, fishing, tennis, and a rousing hand of poker. As often as his schedule allowed, he indulged his love of these sports. Once, after he had retired, he negotiated a guided fishing trip to Alaska as an honorarium for presenting a commencement address.

While he was working, the easiest of these outlets to access was tennis. The sport served as both a mental and physical catharsis for him. As part of an article on handling stress, Priest explained to the reporter, "If something's eating at me and I can't find an answer, I find if I play an hour and a half of tennis and knock the hell out of that ball, I can come back and find a solution. I become more competent analytically if I just sweep everything away."[34] Indeed, he turned his mind fully to the game. He was very competitive.

Ed Gleazer remembered playing doubles with Priest as his partner. Gleazer said he was approaching the game as recreation. Finally Priest shouted to him, "GLEAZER – HIT THE DAMN BALL!"[35] It was Gleazer's estimation that he'd not been playing with the vigor Priest felt he should. Giving that as a single example, Gleazer said he learned from Priest that each task should be attacked with energy and determination, and he remembered those very simple but pointed words when special effort was needed in his job.

After observing Priest on the tennis court while shadowing him for material for an article in *Scene Magazine* in 1971, a reporter from the *Dallas Morning News* described Priest's game as "playing for blood." She said he played from the gut "with the gusto and determination of a Wimbledon finalist."[36] Priest admits he is a vehement competitor in all things. Tennis is a safe way to release steam, but his main objective is to win.

He was chagrined when at seventy-seven, he injured his knee while playing tennis and was doubly miffed that the healing process would keep him off the courts for an undetermined number of months. After a variety of treatments and physical therapy, the final prognosis was no more tennis—ever. He had lost his physical outlet for negative feelings and summarily warned everyone he was going to be permanently testy.

The very fact he joked about his physical condition and predicted lack of pleasantness was an indication that while tennis had been a release valve for him, it was not essential. His true balance and sense of inner peace came from the depth of his understanding of what is real and what is worthy of emotional energy; everything is more palatable when tempered with humor.

In seeking balance in his life, Priest revered the importance of a good home life. He once told a reporter for the *Dallas Morning News,* "I don't see how a person can carry on effectively in a high pressure executive role if he has to go home and listen to a shrew everyday. My home situation has been as tranquil as any I know. . . . We communicate. We have mutual respect."[37] The other part of "we" was the beautiful girl who rode a horse past his home when he was a boy. Marietta Shaw had been his wife for thirty-three years when he gave the reporter that description of his marriage.

Margaret McDermott became good friends with the Priests and she said that Marietta had been one of Priest's great strengths. Marietta was also described as absolutely honest. They did not use their honesty to berate each other on points of imperfection, but rather to settle differences and to encourage and support each other. They had each grown up in homes filled with yelling and quarreling. They promised each other to approach unavoidable differences with discussion. The evolution of communication that transpired over the years of marriage created phrases, or little expressions that indicated it was time to close the debate and move on. They developed a "chit" system. When one person felt particularly strong about an issue, he or she would ask to "cash in a chit." That meant the person wanted to go ahead with the idea, or decision without mutual agreement on the points. It was an agreement to disagree, and to harbor no hard feelings.

Priest gave much credit to Marietta for his success. In his estimation, he could not have done all that he did or progress to the level of chancellor without her never waning support. At his retirement celebration, he praised her as "always a tower of strength when I needed support, which was often."[38]

There was also a united front in child rearing. They supported each other in decisions concerning their only son, Andy. By their example, he never tried to play them against each other. Andy was an example of one of the purposes of community colleges. As a youngster, he demonstrated an aptitude in mechanical skills. He attended El Centro and a General Motors mechanics school. By the time the Eastfield auto mechanics program was in place, the young Priest had already completed his bachelor's degree at the University of North Texas (then North Texas State University) where he graduated with honors. Andy taught in the automotive technology program at Eastfield College and occasionally served as a consultant and expert witness in vehicle collisions, giving analysis of the wreckage and physical evidence at the scene. Eventually he moved into consulting full-time.

Andy is much taller than his father, but his voice and form of expression clearly reveal his heritage. Andy has two children. The oldest, Matt, has a master's degree from the University of Texas at Dallas in finance computer programming. Jill is completing her doctorate in paleontology at Oregon State University. Priest is close to his family. It is not unusual for Andy to stop by just because he is in the neighborhood. Matt and Jill visit their grandfather when they can and telephone often.

Priest's one regret regarding his family is that he was not more involved and supportive of Andy's educational pursuits. The old adage of the preacher's kid being the least well behaved may hold true in other professions as well. Priest indicated he was so occupied with ensuring quality education for everyone else's child that he did not attend well enough to his own. Andy attained a high level of graduate education as well as professional success, and Priest is proud of him, but wishes he had verbalized it more along the way. That would be the one point of imbalance in his professional and personal life.

Even though Priest did not unduly burden his wife with the

problems of the work day, there has to be some influence of personal life on professional life and vice versa. In selecting their new home in Texas, the Priests considered the social demands of Priest's new job. They were given immediate social prominence by the caliber of the board who had selected him. Sought by the social editors of both major daily newspapers, Marietta had the responsibility of explaining their lifestyle and how it was reflected in the house that they would choose. She emphasized their preference for casual living. She detailed features, "I look for an open living area, like a living room-den combination, perhaps with a wood burning fireplace: sort of an indoor-outdoor feeling."[39] The house they bought near White Rock Lake personified those words, and Priest repeated those sentiments some twenty-nine years later in retelling their house-hunting goals. His view, although the same in physical description of the desired features in a house, was a much more analytical and practical one. Knowing all the business related functions that would be part of his new job, Priest wanted a house with few corners or nooks. In talking about the house they chose, he said, "One of the nice things about the design is it keeps the group flowing. As one comes in the door, the rest move right on into the next room. There's always an escape route so some guy can't get you cornered who is looking for a job for his nephew or somebody."[40]

Indeed, the house meanders from space to space with partial walls and large walkthrough areas in the main part of the home. There is a wood-burning fireplace in the living-den area. The back wall is an expanse of windows visually bringing inside the densely treed backyard. The décor is an eclectic collection of personal treasures, art, and artifacts from a lifetime of varied experiences and travels. Marietta had furnished the house with the philosophy that "Anything is compatible if you like it."[41]

Marietta was a constant part of Priest's life for forty-eight years. She died in 1989 after a courageous battle with cancer. Seeking solace in the most peaceful of the sports he loved, Priest went fishing with a friend of his who was a preacher. The quiet of a lake can lend itself to introspection, and the conversation turned to speculation about remarriage. Priest indicated he thought that would be disrespectful of Marietta. The preacher ensured him that quite the opposite was true. People who remarried after the death of a spouse were affirming it had been a happy experience that they wanted to have again.

Ann Sparks had worked in the district for many years. She was newly widowed and at that time working as the secretary to the president of Richland College, Steve Mittlestet. Priest, as chancellor emeritus, maintained an office at Richland. He and Ann had many occasions for conversation and they shared many of the same friends. After a brief courtship, the two married on January 23, 1990, less than two years after Marietta's death. Priest told friends in jest and somewhat in truth, "If someone my age wants to get married, he can't take a long time making the decision."[42]

Since Priest's life with Ann began nearly ten years after his retirement from the district, it gave them a very different framework for their relationship but had the added challenge of a blended family. They live in the same house he and Marietta shared. That is often a difficult setting for a new wife, but Ann seems as at ease there, as if she had personally selected it to establish a home for her new marriage. Priest compliments her for gently placing her personal touch in the décor of the house without eradicating the life that had been shared before. Priest extols her for her loving support and generous heart.

Ann's adaptability goes without saying. While the work and social demands are not the same as when Priest was chancellor, there are many work related functions they must attend. Ann knows most people in the district, but Priest is still in the spotlight as the founding chancellor. Once, this author apologized for calling her Ann and referring to him always as Dr. Priest. She smiled and replied, "No apology necessary. I'm used to it." The response was not one of "poor me," but of gracious understanding of his role and hers in the public arena. Privately they are in concert as a couple. They have differing views on some matters, she being less conservative. Discussions might turn lively, but never destructive. It is apparent they each have great insight into the intricacies of relationships both personal and professional.

CHAPTER EIGHT

Retirement

The End of an Era

By 1980, the Dallas County Community College District had grown from a concept and to the fourth largest community college district in the country. Seven college campuses had been built placing every citizen in Dallas County within fifteen minutes driving time from a campus. That surpassed the "twenty-minute driving time" promise made to the North Dallas Chamber of Commerce in 1965. Even that was ten minutes shorter than the nationally considered optimum of thirty minutes. The technical/vocational certificate and degree programs offered by the DCCCD had grown from the initial thirteen offered by El Centro to a district-wide 121 programs, with an overall job placement rate of ninety percent of graduates. The roster of academic transfer courses had strengthened and over half of the students in the district's colleges transferred to four-year colleges and universities. The district had also grown in its support of workforce education and personal enrichment through the less traditional non credit mode of continuing education courses. Collectively the colleges served almost eighty-thousand students, of whom, 43,400 were in the credit programs.

Priest had realized the correctness of his early career decision to move from his childhood dream of being a high school history teacher to working in community colleges. He had lived up to the expectation of the founding board of the DCCCD, and he had kept his promise to the residents of Dallas County. Priest was not yet sixty-five. With all going so well, and a salary that still topped all of the other state government leaders, why did he choose 1980 as the year to retire?

The reasons for Priest retiring when seemingly all was well with the city, the county, the district, the board, and their constituents, were explained publicly and privately. In his formal request for retirement which was submitted to the Board of Trustees, Priest listed three reasons for wanting to retire. First he wanted more time for some personal goals, a commonly cited reason for retirement of chief executive officers of both public and private organizations. Priest also indicated that he had less energy than the demand of the job warranted. The last reason was perhaps the most cogent. In his estimation, there was a need for a change in the leadership in order to meet the changing dynamics of the job. He further explained in his written request, "I am convinced the time for change is here for me and much more importantly for the job."[1] Privately, he shared with colleagues that he realized that new styles of leadership were moving into the mainstream of administration and at sixty-three he was not likely to change. He made it quite clear, he felt it was time for a revitalization of the position from fresh perspectives.

In a video-taped interview just a few days before his official retirement date, Priest again talked about the demands of the job requiring the energy of a forty- or fifty- year-old. He explained that he had watched "old goats" in the field of higher education stay on the job beyond their period of usefulness, and he was quite adamant about not wanting to do that. Between the lines is the unspoken desire to leave while on top, but Priest's list of reasons and explanations also reveal a man with a realistic view of himself.

During his tenure as chancellor of the Dallas County Community College District, Priest accumulated many awards and honors of national scope, including his election in 1978 to the top educational post in the country as chairman of the board of the American Council of Education (ACE), the national coordinating body for all post-secondary education, and the position of their board chair is typically held by a university president or chancellor. Priest published fourteen articles and served in more than twenty-eight civic and professional organizations and boards.

In 1980, after he announced his retirement, there was a surge of awards and recognitions to honor and celebrate a lifetime of contributions and service to education. He was profiled repeatedly as a national leader in the community college movement. In a letter to the Association of Community College Trustees, Dallas County Community College District board member, Pattie Powell said, "To his board, his colleagues, and his community, he epitomizes the best that a professional educator can be. Bill Priest is a straight-talking, clear-thinking, forward-looking man of action. His career in education spans forty years, with more than thirty years devoted to the advancement of the community college."[2] Those words placed Priest in nomination for the prestigious Marie Y. Martin Award for national impact on community college education. He won that award.

R. Jan LeCroy, vice chancellor of academic affairs and Priest's successor, nominated Priest for the Mirabeau B. Lamar Medal for having "played a major role in the healthy growth and development of the community college concept in Texas."[3] Again, Priest was the recipient of the honor.

In the civic arena, Jerry Gilmore, chairman of the Board of Trustees of the DCCCD, nominated Priest for the Linz Award. This annual award is presented to the resident of Dallas County judged to have conferred the greatest benefit on Dallas through volunteer work. Gilmore acknowledged that Priest's "good deeds" were not limited to a year, but explained that the "county has benefited immeasurably from his vision, his leadership and his boundless energy."[4] Priest did not win the Linz Award. In later years, Priest indicated he was not a likely candidate for that award because any benevolent work he had done was in the line of his job and would not be considered "volunteer." Priest, however, continued to add to his roster of recognitions by being inducted into the Athletic Hall Of Fame at the University of California at Berkeley shortly after his retirement.

All of these honors and awards added to his already impressive professional vita, but none were as meaningful to Priest as being selected as chancellor of the Dallas County Community College District. It is a rare and golden treasure when a person considers the job for which one is chosen as an honor, an award, and doing the job as a reward in itself.

On January 15, 1981, Priest officially retired. The district administrators and faculty held a luncheon in tribute to him and to celebrate his career. The group of some seven hundred people gathered at Mountain View College. The gym was filled with long tables draped with white clothes. They had been arranged banquet style facing a portable stage complete with lectern and microphone for a variety of presentations.

It had been decided some months before that each college would make a scrapbook for him including the history and highlights of that college. The president of each college was to make a formal presentation of the scrapbook to Priest at the luncheon. Floyd Elkins, the president of Cedar Valley College, was hospitalized a few days before the event. The campus administrators and faculty selected the director of Public Information, the position that I held at that time, to represent the campus and present the scrapbook to Priest. I had been a full-time employee with the district only four years, but I was the one who had prepared the scrapbook. I felt quite inadequate to speak on behalf of higher level administrators with many more years in the district, and the situation was even more intimidating because I knew I would be among the presidents of the district, there to honor the top person in the district, in front of the top leadership in the district. In my thinking, I had no words appropriate for such an auspicious occasion, from such an inauspicious person. The presentations were made in order of the opening of the colleges. Cedar Valley College was fifth. I walked up the steps, across the platform, stood on the left side of Priest and said, "We are very sorry that Dr. Elkins could not be here today, but if he were, he could not do this." Handing Priest the scrapbook, I leaned in and kissed him on the cheek. The audience erupted in applause and laughter. The tough-talking, straight-shooting autocrat stood blushing and for a few moments speechless.[6]

Employees from the district Office made one of the last presentations. The group gathered on stage bedecked in the T-shirts imprinted with "A Legend in His Own Time." With great ceremony, Priest was presented with his own T-shirt neatly folded in a box. As he unfolded it, again the audience broke into applause and laughter as they read, "A Legend in His Own Mind."

Priest was also presented with a engraved plaque from North Lake College. Placed prominently at the top of the plaque was a butterfly bow tie, Priest's trademark. He confessed that he never learned how to tie a bow tie. His wife or his secretary always had that task. His staff used to tell him he needed to add that to the job description of his secretary. Along with organization and typing skills he should add, "ability to tie a bow tie."

There were some serious presentations but all had varying degrees of levity. When the podium was turned over to Priest for his remarks, he said, "I know we've placed creativity high on the list of factors influencing our employment decision—but until today, I had no idea how successful we have been. . . . I loathe stuffiness, so this effort has to be rated 4.0."[5] Reaching into the inside pocket of his sports jacket, he said that flying back to Dallas the day before, it occurred to him he wanted to acknowledge several people in the district with whom he had worked closely. He then proceeded to compliment and roast several administrators and faculty members. He read from a list of things for which he was grateful and at the top was "the opportunity to have been in the right place at the right time to have a piece of the action in putting together the greatest community/junior college project ever attempted."[7]

Priest retired with the title of chancellor emeritus and remained as a consultant to the board. He assisted in various matters of historical reference and in surveys of facility planning. He was the primary consultant for assisting the board in information gathering during the national search for chancellor after Larry Tyree resigned and returned to Florida in 1989. He continued to serve as a liaison for the district with Dallas leadership who had worked with Priest for a number of years. That work with the district continued for twenty years.

At the age of eighty-three, the same vision and objectivity about himself that had led him to retire remained keenly in place. In January, 2001, Priest closed his office at the Richland College campus stating he would no longer serve as a consultant to the district because he felt he was approaching a time when his analysis might not be as acute and his awareness of new directions were not as current. Although he withdrew from a position of formal consultant, there are many in higher education from board members to college presidents to deans who still seek his counsel privately. His influence continues and his insights are as revered as thirty years ago. It is difficult for his protégés and colleagues to let him completely retire.

CHAPTER NINE

Legacies

The word legacy by definition denotes something transmitted by or received from an ancestor or predecessor from the past. It is derived from the middle English and middle French word, legate. A legate is an official emissary. It is akin to the word legend which is a story or body of stories coming down from the past. Not part of the word form, but definitely part of a legacy are monuments defined as evidence of someone notable, the placement of a stone or a building erected in remembrance of a person. The legacies of Bill Priest represent all three definitions. His legacy, in many ways, bequeathed to future generations all that he contributed to the development of community colleges. He mentored, gave opportunities to, and otherwise helped to develop a number of educational emissaries. Finally, in tribute to all that he did, several "monuments" carry his name.

Many of the elements of higher education that Priest transmitted to current students began in California: the associate degree in nursing, televised courses, and non credit courses; but these were honed and expanded during his tenure in Dallas. At the time of his retirement, DCCCD board member Pattie Powell spotlighted some of Priest's accomplishments. She credited Priest with being a true advocate for adult learning by offering a healthy schedule of courses, both credit and non credit, in the evenings. Non credit courses have always been coordinated through a separate department. In expanding outreach services, each of the seven colleges have added a corporate training or workforce education arm in which non credit instruction is designed specifically for the company. Those classes are often held on site at the company.

Powell further lauded Priest for blazing "the trail for developmental studies in the mid-sixties."[1] In the state of Texas, developmental courses became more important after the state added its own test for entering freshman with required remediation until all sections of the TASP test area were passed. English as a second language has been added to the developmental roster to assist the increasing number of immigrants and international students. Over one hundred countries are represented among the students in the DCCCD.

The movement of nursing education from the hospitals to colleges is called by some, the most important change in higher education in the twentieth century. It certainly has proven to be a positive for the field of medical care since the associate degree nursing program in community colleges is the primary supplier of registered nurses in the country.

Others call distance education, which began with televised courses and has extended to courses offered on the internet, as the most significant innovation in higher education. Priest was one of the early pioneers in the area, piloting a live broadcast government course in California. It was in the DCCCD where he supported the development of the concept to a national standard. Shortly after his retirement in 1981, the Instructional Television name was changed to the Center for Telecommunications. By 1989, it was touted as the community college leader in offering courses via television. That same year, the district built a new facility for the production of telecourses with state of the art studios. One studio was designed specifically for instruction via live broadcasts to multiple sites with interactive capabilities permitting students to ask questions of the instructor during the broadcast. The teaching studio also allowed the instructor to be the director, as they could switch from a front shot camera, or to an overhead camera, to running a video tape. The new facility, located on the northwest side of the Richland College campus, was named the R. Jan LeCroy Center for Educational Telcommunications. LeCroy was selected as chancellor after Priest's retirement. LeCroy continued and increased support for distance learning. The LeCroy Center staff has won numerous awards for excellence from the National University Telecommunications Network. They offer professionally produced courses via PBS and cable networks, sell their courses to clients in the United States and thirty foreign countries, and now participate in the Global Learning Network with on-line courses. In the late 1990s, DCCCD and thirty other education institutions created a virtual institution called the Western Governors University, and the DCCCD is the only community college system in Texas that participates.

While there is variance in the minds of people as to the single innovation that could be called Priest's greatest contribution to higher education, there is concurrence among professionals in the field that establishing the Dallas County Community College District and developing it into a national model is at the top of the list, and that it had a profound effect on the community college movement. Terry O'Banion, the first full-time president of the League for Innovation, said, "as the district grew, every new building, every new instructional program set a national standard."[2] Dale Parnell, former President of the American Association of Community and Junior Colleges, evaluated the DCCCD from two perspectives: as president of the national organization for all two-year institutions of higher learning and as chancellor of a multi-college district. In the mid 1970s, as chancellor of San Diego Community College District, Parnell and his Board of Trustees made a benchmark trip to Dallas to study the innovations in instruction and the creative approaches to effectively running a multi-college district. From a national viewpoint, Parnell called the DCCCD a model. He said it helped to set the direction for the growth and development of junior colleges into comprehensive community colleges. For the establishment of this model, Parnell gave credit to Priest. He said, "Priest went to Texas with several years experience, some great ideas and built that [Dallas County] district from nothing. It quickly took the lead in innovations over older institutions and became a national model."[3] Parnell specified Santa Fe Community College and San Juan College in Farmington, New Mexico as two colleges that looked to the DCCCD as a model for their development.

The facilities themselves were innovations for the time. Each campus won a variety of architectural awards for design. The farsightedness of Priest and the founding board for purchasing what some thought was too much land for each campus was indeed appropriate. Each college continues to add programs and buildings. Advances in technology and the increase in students both call for additional space. In the spring of 2002, the DCCCD hit an all time record enrollment of 54,702 in credit classes and an additional 32,296 in non credit continuing education courses. The growth in population around each of the campuses and the escalating cost of land makes additional land purchases prohibitive.

A less obvious remaining effect in the district is the attitude of expected innovation, creativity, and risk taking. Priest led by example in taking risks and being the first to try a new medium for instruction or accept students branded by much of higher education as "not college material." He demanded innovation from those who worked for him reminding them that nothing moves forward without some risk-taking in new efforts. That expectation quietly resounds in the college halls today. "But we've always done it this way," or "That's never been done before," are unacceptable reasons for not trying a new idea. Resting on previous successes is not allowed. The striving for continuous quality improvement and better ways of doing whatever the process is, keeps the DCCCD a vibrant and stimulating place to work and learn.

The continued growth and successes of the various entities of the DCCCD is a testament to its value even without the verbal laurels from educational professionals throughout the country. Priest himself designates the building of the DCCCD as his greatest contribution to education, but without taking much personal credit. Thirteen years after his retirement when he was asked what he thought was his best accomplishment in his career, he answered, "Being privileged to play a lead role in the development of the Dallas County Community College District at a crucial time in community college history and education in this area, and nationally. I was fortunate to be in the right place at the right time doing something I knew a good bit about, in a place where I had tremendous positives going for me to do what needed to be done. This unquestionably is my Mona Lisa. This is the thing which I think is head and shoulders above other things I did. Of course, this broke down into many, many, pieces. But to generalize, being permitted to lead the charge of the development of community colleges in this megalopolis was it, and I got a lot of credit for things anyone could have done, but I did them and I did them well and so I got credit for them."[4]

According to Margaret McDermott, who was there from the beginning, "Without Bill Priest there would not have been a Dallas County Community College District. He's a hero."[5] In an interview five years after he had retired as DCCCD chancellor, R. Jan LeCroy, Priest's successor, echoed the sentiments of many, "By building this exemplary district, that's a huge contribution. To take all [Priest's] experience and background resources and build this district as a model, that's his primary contribution."[6]

While Priest thought it his good fortune to be chosen as the chancellor to assist in building the new Dallas district, he did not take it lightly, nor did he indicate it was an easy task even with all of the support from the board and the ample funding package they had acquired. He stated quite frankly, "I worked my tail off. I did everything I could to make it happen, but the beauty is sometimes you do that and nothing happens. This time, I did it and a lot of good things happened."[7]

Indeed, "a lot of good things happened" and continue to happen. Powell, who remains on the DCCCD Board of Trustees and has served as chair, summed up Priest's forty-two-year career by saying, "The innovation in which Bill Priest has been a prime mover reads today like a text of community college fundamentals. The innovations of this era have rapidly passed into standard practice in community colleges across the country."[8] In a review of current community college literature, such as American Association of Community Colleges' 2000 publication, *The Knowledge Net, A Report of the New Expectations Initiative*, one finds recommended practices and new directions built on the rudiments of those early principles and innovations of the Dallas County Community College District.

The valuable contributions that Priest made to other community colleges through his role as chancellor of the DCCCD is well documented, but locally the impact was much broader than a good higher educational system. In 1978, after Brookhaven College, the final campus of the district, was opened, an editorial by J. Wright ran in the *Dallas Morning News* praising the value to the area. He wrote, "The people of Dallas County have just finished building what may be considered the most enriching possession of all—our community college system."[9]

The boundless benefit to the citizens of Dallas County and the county's economic development was detailed by Jerry Gilmore, board chair in 1981. He said, "In no small way, it has been the hand of Bill Priest which has opened the door to higher education for thousands upon thousands of Dallas County citizens who would otherwise have been locked out by finances, distance, or insurmountable entrance requirements. This opportunity has been significant not only to the many who have enrolled as students, but to all county residents who have enjoyed the by-products of an enhanced environment for business and industry, cultural centers within easy driving distance, and the countless intangible benefits that accrue to an educated citizenry."[10] Those by-products are not only still being produced by the Dallas district, but also continue to grow and improve.

There is close interaction between the employees at the colleges and the communities' Chambers of Commerce, civic and service clubs, city governments and independent school districts. Community leaders serve on the advisory boards for educational programs at the colleges, and college faculty, staff, and administrators serve on boards and committees in the communities. College representatives often assist city and chamber members in recruiting new businesses to the area. The colleges offer quality cultural events by students and host professional performers with low cost tickets for the community. The community colleges today are much more than educators of the citizens to help build a skilled work force. The comprehensive community college is a participating member of the community. This is the philosophy set forth by Priest in the articles he authored in the late 1950s and repeated in future writings and many speeches.

Priest was revered by the business community and the leaders in Dallas and its surrounding suburbs. He had a close working relationship with all the elements that come together in a metropolitan area. Founding president of El Centro, Don Rippey described Priest as an integral part of the development and growth of the city of Dallas as were the Thornton family, the Caruths, the Hunts, Earl Cabell, and Stanley Marcus. In an interview in 1994, Rippey said, "Priest was one of the almost mythical people that built Dallas. Even today, he has that image which is rare."[11]

All of his ideas, philosophies, and innovations that culminated in the Dallas County Community College District are unarguably Priest's legacy as something transmitted by a predecessor from the past. What of the legate, an official emissary, the person to carry the message and the mission forward? These are the people Priest mentored or indirectly influenced in their professional growth. Many people cited the hiring and the development of people as one of Priest's strengths. Claudia Robinson noted that Priest was a good observer of human nature and could quickly size up a person's strengths and weaknesses. One of Priest's adages was "first rate people hire first rate people."[12] This meant the hire at the first level could influence the quality of hires throughout that division. This stress on quality which Priest primarily judged through past accomplishments did not mean he would not allow for weaknesses and mistakes. He expected employees to compensate for weak areas and to learn from mistakes. Another

Priest axiom was that "the only dumb mistakes are those you make twice."[13] Allowing the first mistake was indicative of Priest's high value on risk-taking and he looked for that quality when he was hiring.

Priest agreed with that estimation from others. He regarded himself to be "a pretty good people picker."[14] The characteristics he looked for in a applicant were dedication, stability, loyalty, perseverance, insight, being a self-starter, being a team player, willingness to pull their own weight, and undeveloped leadership ability. He believed that accomplishments are a good indicator of an employee's abilities, but viewed in isolation could skew the data. He felt a person could be quite productive at one level, but ineffectual at a single level higher because of a new set of demands. He also believed that the reverse could be true and a mediocre performer at a lower level might move up where their particular attributes would be a good fit. Robinson felt that her interview with Priest was the best and most thorough she had ever had.

Those interview skills and observations of people's performances often surpassed their own expectations of themselves. Deon Holt was a journalism major and had worked with Priest at Los Rios Junior College District in Sacramento, California. He had split responsibilities teaching journalism and handling public relations duties for the district. Priest called him from his new job in Dallas and asked Holt to join his team as vice president of Planning and Development. This was not a career direction Holt had ever imagined for himself and was quite a leap from teaching and public relations. Priest indicated he knew Holt to be bright, trainable, and capable of learning whatever he needed to. Holt accepted the position, did an excellent job, and later served as the first president of Richland and then the first president of Brookhaven. Again he did well in the role of president at each college. Ironically, one of his most public mistakes was in the area of journalism. As the new president of Richland, he oversaw the production of the first catalogue. This would allow him to draw on his primary education and experience, and also expedite the process. He proofed carefully at each phase, and the day the published books arrived, he noticed his mistake. In the listing of administrators, under "president," Deon's name was listed as "Leon."[15]

In 1982 Holt left the district, returning to California to take the position of chancellor of the Mira Costa College District in Oceanside. He attributed success in his own career to following Priest's example and advice. Specifically he noted his philosophies of hiring the best, never making the same mistake twice, and holding your staff to that same standard; above all, he cited Priest's example of the "care and feeding of the board." Holt called Priest masterful in that sometimes delicate working relationship.

Another person's career influenced by Priest was that of Linda Timmerman. In 1975, Priest was without a secretary. Timmerman was at that time the secretary to the president of Mountain View. She was at home on maternity leave when Priest telephoned her. Most of the conversation that transpired might have been considered politically incorrect or even illegal by today's standards, but Timmerman took no offense and heard it as forthright, clear, and fair, and Priest expected the same from her. He indicated she had a good reputation and he did not want to have to break in someone new to the district. He also made it clear that he believed new babies should not be left in a daycare facility and if she was willing to take the job, he was willing to give her a salary that would cover the cost of in-home care for her child. He did not want an immediate answer, and encouraged her to discuss it with her husband. The implication was when he got an answer, he wanted it to be based on thorough consideration and to be definite. She appreciated his honesty on every count and she accepted the position.

Priest gave Timmerman opportunities she had not expected, such as attending the formation meetings of the League for Innovation to "just be a fly on the wall and observe."[16] In daily operations, Timmerman noticed how he genuinely cared about every person in the district. He once cancelled classes at all the campuses because there was a forecast of an ice storm by mid-day. Texas ice storms are more treacherous than the more common snows of northern states. Not a cloud appeared in the sky that day, and he took criticism for the decision. The next day, he did not cancel classes and the storm arrived in full-force. Then he took criticism for that decision. Making a closure decision in advance of the arrival of severe weather is always difficult. Priest tried to protect and be fair to the staff and students, but he also had a deep sense of protecting the taxpayer's money. Although Priest describes himself as having a temper, Timmerman indicated she never saw him angry, only disappointed. He wrote in her evaluation one year that if she were given the opportunity to get a degree she would become a high level administrator.

Timmerman left the district in September of 1978. By 1981 she had a bachelor's degree, by 1985 her master's, and by 1991 she earned her doctorate of education. In route to her doctorate, she asked for Priest to write a recommendation for her. Priest reports that she asked, "Would you lie for me one more time?" Priest was quick to add, "No lies were necessary for that lady."[17]

Timmerman is currently the vice president of Institutional Advancement at Navarro College in Corsicana, Texas. She reports that daily she uses things she learned from Priest. He taught her to discern between personal and professional remarks by others, and that the leader does not have to know it all. She learned from him not to micro manage and to give authority away when possible. Timmerman indicated that from Priest's example, she learned the whole foundation for moral leadership and that is what good leadership is based on.[18]

Not as drastic a change as for Holt or Timmerman, Steve Mittlestet, president of Richland College, counts himself among those in whom Priest saw a potential that he had not seen in himself. Mittlestet was the dean of Continuing Education when Priest asked him to come to the district office to serve in a combined role of being his assistant, and overseeing certain aspects of planning and development and instructional television. Mittlestet was taken aback. His career goal had been vice president of Instruction at the college level. That was the focus of his education and his experience. He never saw himself in a district office role. Looking back, Mittlestet concurred that Priest was right. The broad scope of those duties was better experience and prepared him for the presidency. He learned things from a district perspective, as well as a campus perspective, and learned about the complexities of a college's physical plan. Priest believes a college president needs to be a generalist who then hires the specialists. Mittlestet learned the value of that philosophy. Under Mittlestet's leadership, Richland College has evolved into a premier community college and consistently leads the other colleges in enrollment.

Priest's emissaries are not limited to employees of the district who worked directly under his supervision. The National Institute for Staff and Organizational Development (NISOD) is an annual conference for community college professionals coordinated by the Community College Leadership Doctoral Program at the University of Texas in Austin. In the general assembly at the 1991 NISOD conference, John Rouche, who succeeded C. C. Colvert as the Director of that program, credited Bill Priest for the success of NISOD. That seemingly was a far stretch until he explained. In 1977, Rouche was planning a community college consortium that would focus on improving instruction, retention, and student success. He called together an advisory committee of community college presidents and chancellors. Most of the presidents on the committee and the faculty at the University of Texas program thought the event should be held in the fall to kick-off the year and to motivate and inspire teachers. Priest was the sole abstainer. According to Rouche, he "gave a lengthy, but focused, presentation on why the NISOD conference should be at the end of the school year rather than the beginning"[19] His point was that faculty would have a freer schedule to attend and the event could be a celebration of a successful school year. He also pointed out to his colleagues that there was usually money left at the end of the spring semester to allow each college to send more people. The conference was scheduled for May at the close of the spring semester and has become one of the best-attended conferences for community college professionals. Numerous faculty and administrators from the DCCCD attend the NISOD conference and several have earned doctorates from the University of Texas

Community College Leadership Program. Like a pebble tossed in a lake, the ripple effect of ideas shared touches many educators for years to come.

The reputation of the DCCCD has always attracted excellent applicants from across the country. That was part of the attraction for Alice Villadsen, vice president of Central Piedmont College in Charlotte, North Carolina, when she applied for the President's position at Brookhaven College in 1997. She was hired and officially assumed the post in July of 1998. Villadsen was delighted to learn that Bill Priest was still involved with the district. She explained, "Upon becoming president in the Dallas district, I was surprised and amazed to discover that Bill Priest, the man himself, was available to me. What a joy it has been to be with him, to enjoy his stories, and to see the still-bright twinkle in his eyes when I report on some good thing about Brookhaven College. He has become a strong mentor and advisor."[20]

The development of emissaries continues, and they occasionally reveal themselves in unexpected places. The DCCCD hosted a reception for the newly named chancellor of the University of North Texas, Lee Jackson, who had served for many years as a county judge in the Dallas area. The event was held in the City Club in downtown Dallas on November 1, 2002. Bill Priest was there with other administrators from the DCCCD and the university. In his remarks, Jackson stated he was pleased to be working at a University that has a doctoral program in higher education named in honor of Bill Priest. He went on to say that Priest had been a friend and supporter for many years, frequently sending him notes of encouragement especially when it was known he was dealing with difficult issues. Completely out of the purview of his role as chancellor, Priest had reached out to a young judge he viewed as worthy of support. That judge moved to the arena of higher education in the very institution teaching and training current and future leaders in community colleges.

The legacy of Priest also warranted a monument, something erected in honor of his accomplishments. There are four places that carry his name, two are in California and two in Texas.

The first place christened with the Priest name was in truth in recognition of the family rather than him. The street that ran in front of his boyhood home in the rural area between French Camp and Stockton was named Priest Lane. Swift Sparks, step grandson of Bill Priest, visited the area to see first hand the corner street sign at the intersection of Priest and French Camp. He presented a framed photograph of the corner complete with street sign to his step grandfather for Christmas that year.

The other three monuments were in tribute to Bill Priest himself. While superintendent of American River Junior College District in Sacramento, Priest oversaw the construction of a new administration building in 1956. After he accepted the position of superintendent of Los Rios Community College District, which was created from a merger of American River and Sacramento City Colleges, the Los Rios Board of Trustees honored Priest by naming the administration building for him. The Bill J. Priest Administration Building is still part of the campus today.

After Priest announced his planned retirement for January 1981 as chancellor of the Dallas County Community College District, the Board of Trustees conducted a national search to fill the position that spring. The vice chancellor of academic affairs, R. Jan LeCroy was selected as the new chancellor. Programs and services continued to be added to the college offerings. Several new areas, all related to working directly with the business community, were put in place in the district by various grant awards. One new division, funded with hard money (i.e. funding that is repetitive, not a one time grant or gift), was The Business and Professional Institute. The purpose of this division was to represent each college to business and industry with direct marketing of credit and non credit courses. In 1987, LeCroy and his successor as vice chancellor, Jack Stone, decided to bring all of these new programs and the long standing Job Training Center (which was at El Centro) under the direction of one administrator. The other grant funded programs included the North Texas Small Business Development Center, and The Center for Government Contracting. Such a combination of similar programs called for a new facility. At the April board meeting, Bob

Bettis, the board chair, announced that the new building would be named in honor of Priest.

A site was selected on the southeast edge of downtown Dallas. Construction took two years and in the intervening time, plans for a Business Incubation Program was added to the mix. Finding a name as an umbrella for the variety of programs to be housed in the new building and that would work well with Bill J. Priest was a challenge. Lengthy discussions and brainstorming sessions were held by those who worked in the various departments and among the top administrators in the district. The building opened in 1989 and was officially named the Bill J. Priest Institute for Economic Development. The length of the name had district employees searching for a shortened version, as is most common with facility names. It was quickly realized that "Priest Institute" could create misunderstandings. Using initials only, BJPIED, was still too long. A shortened set of initials, PIED, could be pronounced as an acronym, but the word conjured up visions of dessert or the Pied Piper of Hamlin. Without discussion, usage through time has evolved into simply the BJP as the reference of choice. The name still causes some confusion on the part of the public. With his name prominently placed across the top of the building and on all of the literature, Priest says that he should be back on the payroll for all of the phone calls for the Institute that he fields at his personal residence.

By 1990, it was decided the institute should carry more than Priest's name in tribute to him. The district archives had a few items, but not enough for a full display. Those in charge of the project approached Priest and asked him to contribute a few more articles. He obliged with an array of trophies and plaques acquired by a lifetime of achievements. A floor to ceiling display case was constructed on the back wall of the foyer at the front entrance of the building. Priest had imagined a small free standing trophy case. When he saw the display, he was impressed with the artistry of the effort and the massive size. He, as is his nature, was humbled by the expansive tribute to him.

The most recent namesake is not a structure, but an educational program, perhaps the most fitting of tributes. In September 2000,

The University of North Texas announced the establishment of the Bill J. Priest Center for Community College Education. The core courses are a cognate of the Higher Education Doctoral Program in the College of Education. The Priest Center for Community College Education also offers conferences, seminars, and a white paper series for community college faculty and administrators.

Naming the center after Priest did not come as an afterthought in order to honor him. In fact, it was his many contributions to community college education and the establishment of the DCCCD in proximity to the university that inspired the creation of a community college doctoral major in the Higher Education Program. A small group began discussing the idea, and as the plan took form, additional University of North Texas administrators became members of the committee. Data gathered demonstrated a need for the program. As there were not many new community colleges being built in the country, existing colleges were growing. There were numerous articles in professional journals pointing to the "graying of the campuses." High percentages of administrators and faculty members are retiring or soon to retire. The need for advanced educational offerings for new administrators and faculty members was apparent. Also, there was a review of other doctoral level programs for community college careers paths. Nationally there were few and some of those were struggling. The strongest program was at the University of Texas in Austin. Great effort was made in the planning of the University of North Texas program to compliment rather than compete with that program. A major difference was the option of a teaching discipline for faculty in conjunction with the community college focused courses.

A formal proposal was presented to the university's top administration and approved. The plans of the committee became reality with a million dollar donation from Don Buchholtz, former DCCCD Board of Trustees member and chair. This generous donation established the Buchholtz Endowed Chair and gave impetus to begin course offerings. An advisory committee of current and former regional community college chancellors, University of

North Texas faculty and administrators, and Bill Priest meet several times a year to hear about progress in the program, reflect on new ideas, and offer guidance.

Above all of the other tributes to Priest, this is the most appropriate. It is not merely a name emblazoned on a sign. It extends the ideologies and benefits of community college education into perpetuity. The program will teach those who will teach and mentor others. It is a befitting commendation for one of the pioneers in community college education.

As of September of 2003, Priest is retired from public life, but has in no way retired from being well-read on current issues in community colleges and the legislative actions that affect them. His counsel is still sought by current leadership in higher education and his ability to engage the interest of an audience of one or one-hundred has not waned.

End Notes

Chapter 1

1. "Bill Priest Knows What He's Doing" article by Lester Grant in the *Stockton Record* from the personal scrapbook of Bill Priest, no page and section numbers from the newspaper.

2. Associated Press article that ran in *San Francisco Examiner* from the personal scrapbook of Bill Priest.

3. The same article as listed in number 2 contained copy from the *Stockton Record*.

4. Ibid.

5. Ibid.

6. Ibid.

7. Priest was interviewed by the author on several occasions in 1994 in preparation for the dissertation and again in 2002 in preparation for this book. Many of the stories were repeated and quotes given more than once; therefore, notes from personal interviews with Priest will not list a specific date.

8. Ibid.

9. Ibid.

Chapter 2

1. Priest, personal interview.

2. President Harry Truman's radio address on the bombing of Hiroshima, *In Our Own Words*, edited by R. Torricelli and A. Cavroll (1999) New York: Kodnsha International.

Chapter 3

1. Priest, personal interview.

2. Douglas, J. A. (2000) *The California Idea and American Higher Education*. Stanford, California: Stanford University Press.

3. Fondiller, S. H. (1983). *The Entry Dilemma: The National League for Nursing and The Higher Education Movement 1952–1972.* New York: National league for Nursing.

4. Priest, personal interview.

5. Data are from the DCCCD District office of Institutional Effectiveness and Research.

6. Ed Gleazer, personal e-mail interview November 2002.

Chapter 4

1. Cohen, A. M. (1969). *Dateline 79: Heretical Concepts for the Community College,* _____Beverly Hills, California: Glencoe Press: Lynes, R. (1966, November) How good are the junior colleges? *Harper's Magazine*; Thornton J. W. Jr. (1966). *The Community Junior College.* New York: John Wiley & Sons, Inc.

2. Gibbons, H. E. (1975). *The Historical Development of the Dallas County Community College District: A Study of Multi-College District.* Unpublished doctoral dissertation, University of Oklahoma, Norman, Oklahoma.; Randolph, W. L. (1974). *An Interpretive Analysis of the Political Process Involved in the Establishment and Development of the Dallas County Community College District: 1964-1974* Unpublished dissertation. University of Texas, Austin, Texas. Unpublished doctoral dissertation, University of North Texas, Denton, Texas; Williams, J. D. (1968). *Major Educational Innovation: A Conceptual Model and a Case-Study Analysis of the Establishment of the Dallas County Junior College.*

3. Williams, Op. Cit. in note 2.

4. Priest, B. J. (1976). "Education" in *The Book of Dallas*, eds. E. Oppenheimer & B. Porterfield, Garden City, New York: Doubleday & Company.

5. Gibbons, Op. Cit., in note 2, Williams, Op. Cit. in note 2

6. Williams, Op. Cit. in note 2.

7. Ibid.

8. Randolph, Op. Cit. in note 2.

9. Williams, Op. Cit. in note 2.

10. Bancroft, B. (1980, December). Community colleges: our last privately run public body. *D Magazine*; Gibbons, Op. Cit. in note 2; Randolph, Op. Cit. in note 2; McDermott, M., personal interview 1994.

11. Randolph, Op. Cit. in note 2.

12. Hoover, D. (1976, November 21). Educator questions worth of higher education. *Dallas Morning News*; Gibbons, Op. Cit. in note 2; Randolph, Op. Cit. in note 2.

13. Williams, Op. Cit. in note 2.

14. Randolph, Op. Cit. in note 2.

15. Gibbons, Op. Cit. in note 2.

16. The Margaret Meade quote was a single page handout at a Total Quality Management workshop for Brookhaven College in November, 1993 conducted by Burt Peachy.

17. McDermott, Op. Cit in note 10.

18. Gibbons, Op. Cit. in note 2; Randolph, Op. Cit. in note 2.

19. Ed Gleazer, personal e-mail interview, November 2002.

20. Priest, B. J., (April, 1965) "Selecting a College President," *AACJC Journal.*

21. Ibid.

22. Ibid.

23. Ibid.

24. Gibbons, Op. Cit. in note 2, Randolph, Op. Cit. in note 2.

25. Ibid.

26. Ibid.

27. Van Cronkhite & Maloy. (1965, August). Press Release available in Priest's personal files.

28. "Poised for Greatness" (December 20, 1965). *Dallas Morning News.*

29. Ibid.

30. Ibid.

31. Priest, personal interview.

32. Ibid.

33. Ibid.

34. Barta, C. (December 5, 1971). "High Priest of Junior Colleges," *Scene Magazine, Dallas Morning News.*

35. Gibbons, Op. Cit. in note 2.

36. Priest, personal interview.

37. Priest, B. J. (August, 1965). "To the People of Dallas." This was the statement Priest prepared for the press kits sent to the media upon his acceptance of the job in the DCCCD.

38. Priest, personal interview.

Chapter 5

1. Newport, D. (1981). *A Program in Community College Leadership: An Interview with Bill J. Priest* [video] Irving , Texas: North Lake College.

2. Holt, D. (1994) a personal interview.

3. Robinson, C. (1994) a personal interview.

4. Kintzer, Jensen, & Hensen. (1969). The multi-institution junior college district. *American Association of Junior Colleges Monograph Series* (from ERIC Clearinghouse for junior college information).

5. Mittlestet, S. (1994) personal interview.

6. Hoover, D. (1966, May 29). College head tells of teachers, campus. *Dallas Morning News.*

7. Holt, Op. Cit. in note 2.

8. Priest, personal interview.

9. Mittlestet, Op. Cit. in note 5.

10. Ibid., Priest, personal interview.

11. Holt, Op. Cit. in note 2.

12 Priest, personal interview.

13. Priest, "Education."

14. Clemons, D. (July 16, 1976). "Two College Chancellors Share some Common Problems, Goals." *The Bakersfield California Scene.*

15. Newport, Op. Cit. in note 1.

16. Rippey, D. (1987). *Some Called it Camelot: The El Centro Story.* Dallas: Subsidy Publication.

17. Rosenberg, L. J. (1978). *Sangers' Pioneer Texas Merchants.* Austin: Texas State Historical Association.

18. Diener, T. (1986). *Growth of an American Invention: A Documentary History of the Junior and Community College Movement.* New York: Greenwood Press.; Rippey, Op. Cit. in note 15; Thornton, J. W., Jr. (1966). *The Community Junior College.* New York: John Wiley & Sons, Inc.

19. LeCroy, R. J. (1994), personal interview; Mittlestet Op. Cit. in note 5.

20. Diener, Op. Cit. in note 17.

21. Priest, personal interview.

22. Ibid.

23. "A Flying Start Near: quick development seen for county college" (May 28, 1966). *Dallas Morning News.*

24. Rippey, Op. Cit. in note 15.

25. Ibid.

26. "Educational Opportunity for War Veterans. (March 22, 1972). *Congressional Record-Senate.* S4503.

27. Rippey, D. (1994) personal interview; Creamer, D. (1994) personal interview.

28. Priest, B. J. (September 1966). "On the Threshold of Greatness." *Junior College Journal.*

29. Hoover, Op. Cit. in note 6.

30. Gehret, K. G. (1972, May 13). Job skills shaped in junior college. *The Christian Science Monitor;* Hoover, Op. Cit. in note 6.

31. Creamer, Op. Cit. in note 26.

32. Rippey, Op. Cit. in note 15.

33. Ibid., Creamer, Op. Cit. note 26.

34. Ibid.

35. Ibid.

36. "Retiring Chancellor Reflects on DCCCD." (September 16, 1980). *The Mesquite Daily News.*

37. Rippey, Op. Cit. in note 26; Creamer, Op. Cit. in note 26.

38. Powell, P. (1980, July). Letter of Nomination for the Marie Y. Martin Award (available in Priest's private files).

39. Barta, C. (1971) *Southwest Scene Magazine, Dallas Morning News*

40. "Bill Priest—man for the job." (August 16, 1964). *The Sacramento Union.*

41. Gibbons, H. E. (1975). *The Historical Development of the Dallas County Community College District.* Unpublished dissertation, University of Oklahoma, Norman, Oklahoma.

42. DCJCD Minutes, November 2, 1965.

43. Priest, personal interview.

44. McDermott, M. (July 19, 1994). Founding member of DCCCD Board of Trustees, personal interview with the author.

45. Priest, personal interview.

46. Ibid., Parsons, C. (1966, October 29). Is teaching an art? Is it a skill? Is it definable? *The Christian Science Monitor.*

47. Mittlestet, S. (1994), personal interview; Priest, personal interview.

48. Ibid.

49. Parsons, Op. Cit. in note 45.

50. Rippey, Op Cit in note 15; LeCroy, Op. Cit. in note 18; Priest, personal interview

51. Priest, personal interview.

52. Newport, Op. Cit in note 1.

53. Weaver, G. (March 9, 1995). Professor of Biology, Eastfield College. Personal interview, Eastfield College, Mesquite, Texas.

54. Bancroft, B. (1980, December). Community colleges: our last privately run public body. *D Magazine.*

55. Priest, B. J. (May 1962). "Do's and Don'ts of Getting Started." *Junior College Journal.*

56. LeCroy, Op. Cit. in note 18; Priest, personal interview.

57. Gleazer, E. (November 27, 2002). President Emeritus of American Association of Community and Junior Colleges. E-mail interview.

58. Ibid.

59. Ibid.

60. O'Banion, T. (1995) personal interview.

61. Priest, personal interview.

62. Priest, B. J. (February 1959). "The Most Significant Problems of Junior Colleges in the Field of Student Personnel Services." *Junior College Journal.*

63. "Poised for Greatness." (December 20, 1965). *Dallas Morning News.*

64. Robinson, C. (1994) personal interview.

65. Ibid.

66, Priest, B. J. (mid-fifties, exact issue date uncertain). Junior College Public Relations, *Nations Schools.*

67. Robinson, personal interview.

68. Priest, personal interview.

69. Priest, B. J. (January 16, 1981). "Retirement Bash Comments." Available in Priest's personal files.

70. Gibbons, Op. Cit. in note 40.

71. Priest, personal interview.

72. Ibid.

73. Bancroft, Op. Cit. in note 53.

74. Priest, personal interview.

75. Bancroft, Op. Cit. in note 53.

76. Gibbons, Op. Cit in note 40.

77. Bancroft, Op. Cit. in note 53.

78. Barta, C. (1971, December 5). High priest of junior colleges. *Southwest Scene Magazine.*

79. Priest, personal interview.

80. Bancroft, Op. Cit. in note 53.

81. Ibid.

82. Priest, Personal interview.

83. Bancroft, Op. Cit. in note 53.

Chapter 6

1. Randolph, W. L. (1974). *An Interpretive Analysis of the Political Process Involved in the Establishment and Development of the Dallas County Community College District: 1964-1974.* Unpublished doctoral dissertation, University of North Texas, Denton, Texas.

2. Priest, personal interview.

3. Poised for greatness. (1965, December 20). *Dallas Morning News.*

4. Newport, D. (1981) *A Program in Community College Leadership: An Interview With Bill J. Priest.* [video] Irving, Texas, North Lake College.

5. McDermott, M. (1994) personal interview.

6. Mittlestet, S. (1994) personal interview.

7. LeCroy, R. J. (1994) personal interview.

8. Griffin, L. & Flick, D. (2003, March 16) Rich past fuels Oak Cliff's comeback, *Dallas Morning News.*

9. Holt, D. (1970) *An Interpretive Analysis of the Developmental Planning of Mountain View College, Dallas Texas.* Unpublished dissertation, University of Texas, Austin, Texas.

10. Ibid.

11. A Flying Start Near: quick development seen for county college. (May 28, 1966). *Dallas Morning News.*

12. Ibid.

13. Holt, Op. Cit. in note 9.

14. Hoover, D. (1994, July 29). College head tells of teachers, campus. *Dallas Morning News.*

15. Holt, D. (1994) personal interview.

16. Priest, personal interview.

17. Ibid.

18. DCJC milestones. (1971, April 17). *Dallas Morning News.*

19. Mittlestet, Op. Cit. in note 6.

20. Neal, J. F. (1990). *The History of the Center for Telecommunications of the Dallas County Community College District.* Unpublished doctoral dissertation, University of North Texas, Denton, Texas.

21. Ibid.

22. Ibid.

23. LeCroy, Op. Cit in note 7.

24. Neal, Op. Cit in note 20.

25. Priest, personal interview.

26. Neal, Op. Cit. in note 20.

27. Ibid.

28. Cohen, A. M. & Brawer, F. B. (1996). *The American Community College.* San Francisco: Josey-Bass Inc.

29. Ogilvie, W. K. & Raines, M. R. (Eds.) (1971). *Perspectives on the Community Junior College.* New York: Appleton Century-Crofts.

30. Priest, personal interview; Mittlestet, Op. Cit. in note 6.

31. Parnell, D. (1995) personal interview.

32. Priest, B. J. & Pickleman, J. E. (1975). *Increasing Production In the Community College: An Action Approach.* AACJC White Paper: Shell Companies Foundation.

33. Clemmons, D. (1976, July 16). Two college chancellors share some common problems, goals. *The Bakersfield California Scene.*

34. Bloom, J. (1976, October 24). A walking tour of El Centro. Is there anything worth saving? *Dallas Times Herald.*

35. Ibid.

36. Priest, personal interview.

37. Bloom, Op. Cit. in note 34.

38. Mittlestet, Op. Cit. in note 6.

39. Priest, personal interview.

40. The words were copied from the plaque that hangs in Priest's office in his home.

41. Fulton, S. (March 20, 1995). Professor of Electronics Technology, Mountain View College. Personal interview, Mountain View College, Dallas, Texas.

42. Ibid.

43. Priest, personal interview.

44. Powell, P. (1980, July). Letter of Nomination for the Marie Y. Martin Award. (Available in Priest's personal files).

45. Holt, D.(1994) personal interview.

46. Flint, J. (2002) personal interview.

47. Hast, K. (December 27, 1976). "Brookhaven Windmill Designed to Blow Your Mind." *Dallas Morning News.*

48. Ibid., Priest, personal interview.

49. Priest, personal interview.

50. Hast, Op. Cit. in note 47.

51. Priest, personal interview; Mittlestet, Op. Cit. in note 6.

52. Hast, Op. Cit in note 47.

53. Mittlestet, Op. Cit in note 6.

54. Priest, personal interview.

55. Fulton, P. (November 3, 1994). Former chancellor of Oakland Community College, Michigan; she is currently an assistant professor at the University of North Texas. Personal telephone interview with the author. Fulton's home, Bloomfield Hills, Michigan.

56. Ibid.

57. Mittlestet, Op. Cit. in note 6.

58. Priest, personal interview.

59. Neal, Op. Cit. in note 20.

60. Robinson, C. (1994) personal interview.

61. Ibid.

62. Ibid.

63. Ibid.

64. Campbell, R. (1994) personal interview.

65. Ibid.

66. Robinson, Op. Cit. in note 60.

67. Bancroft, B. (1980, December). Community colleges: our last privately run public body. *D Magazine*.

68. Priest, personal interview.

69. Ibid.

70. Ibid.

Chapter 7

1. Feist, J. M. (April 9, 1995) "Hail Harry." *Dallas Morning News*.

2. Meachum, B. (March 21, 1995). Professor of Psychology, Cedar Valley College. Personal interview with the author, Cedar Valley College, Lancaster, Texas.

3. Blackshear, R. (June 25, 1994). Instructor, El Centro College. Personal telephone interview. Blackshear's home, Heath, Texas.

4. "Bill Priest of River College—here's one man nobody ever forgets." (May 15, 1960). *The Sacramento Union*.

5. Bancroft, B. (December 1980). "Community Colleges: our last privately run public body." *D Magazine*.

6. Weaver, G. (March 9, 1995). Professor of Biology, Eastfield College. Personal interview with author, Eastfield College, Mesquite, Texas.

7. Meachum, Op. Cit. in note 2.

8. Priest, B. J. (May 1962). "Do's and Don'ts of Getting Started." *Junior College Journal*.

9. Bancroft, *D Magazine.*

10. Gilmore, J. (February 5, 1981). Letter to Linz Award Editor. Available in Priest's
private files.

11. Maccoby, M. (1976). *The Gamesmen.* New York: Simon and Schuster.

12. McCoy, C. (March 27, 1995). Professor of Accounting, Brookhaven College. Personal interview with author. Brookhaven College, Farmers Branch, Texas.

13. Robinson, C. (August 6, 1994). Director of Public Information, DCCCD. Personal interview with author. Crockett's Restaurant, Dallas, Texas.

14. See photo section of this book.

15. Feist, *Dallas Morning News.*

16. "DCJC Milestones." (April 17, 1971). *Dallas Morning News.*

17. Giuliani, R. W. (2002). *Leadership.* New York: Miramax Books.

18. Rippey, D. (July 21, 1994). Retired Professor, Community College Leadership Program, University of Texas. Personal interview with the author. Rippey's home, Austin, Texas.

19. Priest, personal interview.

20. Timmerman, L. (August 7, 2002). Vice President of Institutional Advancement, Navarro Community College. Personal interview with the author. Navarro Community College, Corsicana, Texas.

21. Priest, "Do's and Don'ts" *Junior College Journal.*

22. Robinson, personal interview.

23. "Bill Priest of River College." *Sacramento Union.*

24. Priest, personal interview.

25. Barta, C. (December 5, 1971). "High Priest of Junior Colleges." *Southwest Scene Magazine, Dallas Morning News.*

26. Henderson, L. (November 17, 1974). "Executives and Stress—beating it to the punch." *Sunday Magazine. Dallas Times Herald.*

27. Timmerman, personal interview.

28. "A Flying Start" *Dallas Morning News.*

29. Priest, "Do's and Don'ts." *Junior College Journal.*

30. Priest, B. J. (July 8, 1980). Request for retirement presented to DCCCD Board of Trustees. Available in Priest's private files.

31. Priest, personal interview.

32, Bancroft, *D Magazine.*

33. "Bill Priest of River College." *Sacramento Union.*

34. Henderson, *Dallas Times Herald.*

35. Gleazer, E. (November 27, 2002). President Emeritus of American Association of Community Colleges. E-mail interview.

36. Barta, *Southwest Scene Magazine, Dallas Morning News.*

37. Henderson, *Sunday Magazine, Dallas Times Herald.*

38. Priest, Retirement Bash Comments.

39. Wilson, M. (August 27, 1965). "Mrs. Priest Seeks New Home." *Dallas Times Herald.*

40. Priest, personal interview.

41. Wilson, *Dallas Times Herald.*

42. Robinson, Op. Cit. in note 13.

Chapter 8

1. Priest, B. J. (July 8, 1980) Request for Retirement presented to the DCCCD Board of Trustees. Available in Priest's private files.

2. Powell, P. (July, 1980). Letter of nomination for the Marie Y. Martin Award. Available in Priest's private files.

3. LeCroy, R. J. (October 1980) letter of nomination for the Mirabeau B. Lamar Medal. Available in Priest's private files.

4. Gilmore, J. (February 5, 1981). Letter to Linz Award Editor. Available in Priest's private files.

5. Priest, B. J. (January 16, 1981) Retirement Bash Comments. Available in Priest's private files.

6. During my first interview with Priest, I identified myself by current and past job titles. I further explained that I had made the scrapbook and presented it at his retirement on behalf of Cedar Valley. He filled in the rest of the story because he remembered. I assured him that I had intended no disrespect. He said none had been taken.

7. Priest, Op. Cit. in note 5.

Chapter 9

1. Powell, P. (July 1980). Letter of nomination for Marie Y. Martin Award. Available in Priest's private files.

2. O'Banion, T. (March 24, 1995). president of League for Innovation. Personal telephone interview with author, League for Innovation Office, Mission Viejo, California.

3. Parnell, D. (March 28, 1995). Professor of Higher Education, Oregon State University. Personal telephone interview with author, Oregon State University, Oregon.

4. Priest, personal interview.

5. McDermott, M. (July 19, 1994). Former Founding member Board of Trustees of DCCCD. Personal interview with author. McDermott's home, Dallas, Texas.

6. LeCroy, R. J. (July 19, 1994). President, Dallas Citizen Council. Personal interview with author. Dallas Citizen Council's Office, Dallas, Texas.

7. Priest, personal interview.

8. Powell, Letter of nomination for Marie Y. Martin Award.

9. Barta, C. (December 5, 1971) "High Priest of Junior Colleges." *Southwest Scene Magazine, Dallas Morning News.*

10. Gilmore, J. (February 5, 1981) Nomination letter to Linz Award Editor. Available in Priest's private files.

11. Rippey, D. (July 21, 1994). Retired professor, Community College Leadership Program, University of Texas. Personal interview with author. Rippey's home, Austin, Texas.

12. Robinson, personal interview; Holt, personal interview.

13. Timmerman, personal interview; Holt, personal interview.

14. Priest, personal interview.

15. Holt, D. (July 28, 1994). Chancellor Emeritus, Mira Costa College, Ocean side, California. Personal interview with the author. Lobby of Radisson Inn, Amarillo, Texas.

16. Timmerman, personal interview.

17. Priest, personal interview.

18. Timmerman, personal interview.

19. Rouche, J. (November 15, 2002). Director of the Community College Leadership Program, University of Texas, Austin, Texas. E-mail interview with author.

20. Villadsen, A. (January 30, 2003) President Brookhaven College, Farmers Branch, Texas. E-mail interview with author.

Appendix

Bill Jason Priest Vitae

Education

A.B., M.A., Ed.D.—University of California Berkeley

Post-Doctoral study at Columbia University

Experience

July, 1965-1981

Chancellor, Dallas Community College District

1963-1965

Superintendent, Los Rios Junior College District, Sacramento

1955-1963

Superintendent/President. American River Junior College District, Sacramento

1948-1955

Assistant Superintendent, Orange Coast College District, Costa Mesa, California

Professional Memberships

Chairman, Board of Directors, American Council on Education, 1978-1979

Chairman, Board of Directors, North Park Savings Association

Board of Directors, Servicemen's Opportunity College

Board of Directors, Past President, League for Innovation in the Community College

Finance Center Advisory Committee, Education Commission of the States

Past President, American Association of Community and Junior Colleges

Past President, California Junior College Association

Civic Activities

Board of Directors, United Way of Metropolitan Dallas

Board of Directors, YMCA of Dallas

Board of Directors, City Club of Dallas

Salesmanship Club of Dallas

Junior League Advisory Board

Higher Education Task Force of Goals for Dallas

Vice President, Dallas Council on World Affairs

Leadership Dallas Advisory Council

Advisory Board of the Board of Trustees, Dallas Symphony Orchestra, 1973-1974

Southwestern Medical foundation Development Council

Honors and Awards

Who's Who in American College and University Administration

Who's Who in America, Thirty-seventh edition

Personalities of the South

Leaders in Education, Fifth edition

Dictionary of International Biography, Thirteenth edition, 1976–1977

Press Club "Headliner of the Year" for 1978

North Dallas Chamber of Commerce "Award for Excellence" for 1976

Man of the Year, San Juan, California for 1959

Courtesy of the District Public Information Office, Dallas County Community College District

Publications of Bill J. Priest

"The most significant problems of junior colleges in the field of student personnel services,." *Junior College Journal, 26* (1959, February): 303-306.

"Do's and don'ts of getting started, *Junior College Journal, 32* (1962, May): 268-270.

"Faculty-Administrator Relationships." *American Association of Junior College Journal* (March 1964): 4-8.

"Selecting a College President." *American Association of Junior College Journal* (April 1965): 5-7.

"On the Threshold of Greatness." *American Association of Junior College Journal* (September 1966): 6-8.

"The First Two Years." *The Inercollegean* (orientation issue 1966):5.

"The Financing and Control of Community Colleges." *Compact,* Education Commission of the States (December 1968): 20.

"The Dallas Express." *American Association of Junior College Journal* (March 1972): 12.

"The Dollar Squeeze and the Community College." *Compact,* Education Commission of the States (April 1972).

"Vocations Day—An Effective Group Counseling Device." *American Association of Junior College Journal,* n.d.

"Junior College Public Relations." *Nation's Schools,* n.d.

Priest, B. J. (1969, October). Progress and prospects. *Outlook.* p.3.

Encyclopedia of Education, s.v. "presidency, higher education: community and junior colleges."

Co-authored:

Priest, Bill J. and H. Deon Holt, "How to Organize for Facilities Planning." *American Association of Junior College Journal* (March 1967):30 and *A Primer for Planners,* American Association of Junior College brochure (1967):22.

_____ and H. Deon Holt, "Community College Outlook for the 70s." *Compact,* Education Commission of the States (August 1970): 34.

_____ and Ensile O. Oglesby, Jr., "Selecting the Design Team." *American Association of Junior College Journal* (September 1967):26 and *A Primer for Planners*, American Association of Junior College brochure (1967):13.

_____ and J. E. Pickleman, "Increasing Production In The Community College: An Action Approach." *American Association of Junior College Journal*, White Paper: Shell Companies Foundation.

Unpublished works:

"Administration of Philippine Education Under Commonwealth Government." Master's thesis, University of California at Berkeley, n.d.

"Philippine Education in Transition." Ph.D.diss., University of California at Berkeley, n.d.

Bibliography

Books

American Association of Community Colleges. (2000) *The Knowledge Net, A report of the new expeditions initiative.* Washington, D.C.: Community College Press.

Anderson, G. J. (1990). *Fundamentals of Educational Research.* London: The Falmer Press.

Ary, D., Jacobs, L. C., & Razavich, A. (1985). *Introduction To Research In Education.* New York: Holt, Rinehart & Winston.

Barzun, J. and Graff, H. F. (1985). *The Modern Researcher.* Fourth Edition. New York: Harcourt Brace Jovanovich, Publishers.

Best, J. W. & Kahn, J. V. (1986). *Research In Education.* Englewood Cliffs, New Jersey: Prentice-Hall.

Bogdan, R. C. & Biklen, S. K. (1982). *Qualitative Research For Education: An Introduction to Theory and Methods.* Boston, Mass: Allyn Bacon.

Borg, W. R., & Gall, M. D. (1989). *Educational Research An Introduction.* New York: Longman.

Burgess, R. G.(Ed.) (1985). *Issues in Educational Research: Qualitative Methods.* London: The Falmer Press.

Carver, J. 1990. *Boards That Make a Difference: A New Design For Leadership in Nonprofit and Public Organization.* San Francisco: Jossey-Bass, Inc.

Cohen, A. M. (1969). *Dateline '79: Heretical Concepts for the Community College.* Beverly Hills, California: Glencoe Press.

Cohen, A. M. & Brawer, F. B. (1996). *The American Community College.* San Francisco: Josey-Bass Inc.

Cohen, L. & Lawrence, M. (1980). *Research Methods in Education.* London: Croom Helm.

Denzin, N. K. (1982). *The Research Act.* New York: Praiger.

Diener, T. (1986). *Growth of An American Invention: A Documentary History of the Junior and Community College Movement.* New York: Greenwood Press.

147

Douglas, J. A. (2000). *The California Idea and American Higher Education: 1850 to the 1960 Master Plan.* Stanford, California: Stanford University Press.

Fondiller, S. H. (1983). *The Entry Dilemma: The National League for Nursing and the Higher Education Movement 1952-1972.* New York: National League for Nursing.

Giuliani, R. W. (2002). *Leadership.* New York: Miramax Books

Haase, P. T. (1990). *The Origins and Rise of Associate Degree Nursing Education.* London: Duke University Press.

Jaeger, R. M. (Ed.) (1988). *Complementary Methods for Research in Education.* Washington, D.C.: American Educational Research Association.

Johnson, B. L. (1969). *Inlands of Innovation Expanding: Changes in the Community College.* Beverly Hills, California: Glencoe Press.

Johnston, W. B. (1987). *Workforce 2000: Work and Workers for the 21st Century.* Washington, D.C.: U. S. Department of Labor.

Maccoby, M. (1976). *The Gamesmen.* New York: Simon and Schuster.

O'Banion, T. (1989). *Innovation In The Community College.* New York: Collier McMillan Publishers.

Ogilvie, W. K. & Raines, M. R. (Eds.). (1971). *Perspectives on the Community Junior College.* New York: Appleton Century-Crofts.

Rippey, D. (1987). *Some Called It Camelot: The El Centro Story.* Dallas: Subsidy Publication.

Roseberg, L. J. (1978). *Sangers' Pioneer Texas Merchants.* Austin: Texas State Historical Association.

Sherman, R. R. & Webb, R. B. (Eds.). (1988). *Qualitative Research in Education: Focus and Methods.* London: The Falmer Press.

Spradley, J. P. (1979). *The Ethnographic Interview.* New York. Holt, Rinehard & Winston.

Thornton, J. W., Jr. (1966). *The Community Junior College.* New York: John Wiley & Sons, Inc.

Articles, Chapters, and other Written Works

A Flying Start Near: quick development seen for county college (1966, May 28). *Dallas Morning News.* 8A.

Bancroft, B. (1980, December). Community Colleges: our last privately run public body. *D Magazine,* 136-160.

Barta, C. (1971, December 5). High priest of junior colleges. *Southwest Scene Magazine.* 6-12.

Battle of the Buildings. (1976, October 26). *Dallas Times Herald.* 2C.

Beach, M. (1969). History of education. *Review of Educational Research. 39.* 561-576.

Bill Priest—man for the job. (1964, August 16). *The Sacramento Union.* 2C.

Bill Priest of River College - here's one man nobody ever forgets. (1960, May 15). - *The Sacramento Union.* 30

Bloom, J. (1976, October 24). A walking tour of El Centro. Is there anything worth saving. *Dallas Times Herald,* 1C, 8C.

Bowing out. (1981, January 16). *Irving Daily News.* 10.

Campbell, J. K. (1988). Inside lives: the quality of biography. *Qualitative Research in Education: Focus and Methods.* Sherman, R.R. & Webb, R. B.(Eds). London: The Falmer Press. 59-75.

Chancellor of DCCCD heads education group, (1978, October 14). *Dallas Morning News.* 4A.

Clemmons, D. (1976, July 16). Two college chancellors share some common problems, goals. *Bakersfield California Scene.* 9.

Cook, K. (1991, October). DCCCD at 25: a quarter of a century of growth. *Intercom.* p.5.

Cook, K. (1994, October). Bill Priest honored for lifetime service to community colleges. *Intercom.* p.5.

DCJC milestones. (1971, April 17). *Dallas Morning News.* 2D.

Edson, C. H. (1988). Our past and present: historical inquiry in education. *Qualitative Research in Education: Focus and Methods.* Sherman, R.R. & Webb, R. B.(Eds.) London: The Falmer Press. 44-58.

Feist, J.M. (1995, April 9) Hail Harry. *Dallas Morning News.* 1A.

Flick, D. & Griffin, L. (2003, march 16) Rich past fuels Oak Cliff's comeback. *Dallas Morning News.* 1, 25A.

Gehret, K. G. (1972, May 13). Job skills shaped in junior college. *Christian Science Monitor.* 10.

Hast, K. (1976, December 27). Brookhavem Windmill designed to blow your mind. *Dallas Morning News.* 1D.

Henderson, L. (1974, November 17). Executives and stress - beating it to the punch. *Sunday Magazine, Dallas Times Herald.* 4-8.

High paid priest of higher education. (1980, December). *D Magazine.* 160.

Holding the line. (1970, June 26). *Dallas Morning News.* 4d.

Hoover, Dennis. (1966, May 29). College head tells of teachers, campus. *Dallas Morning News.* 10A.

Hoover, Dennis. (1976, November 21). Educator questions worth of higher education. *Dallas Morning News.* 1AA.

Kaestle, C. F. (1988). Recent methodological developments in the history of American education. *Complementary Methods for Research in Education.* Jaeger, R. M. (Ed.). Washington, D.C.: American Educational Research Association. 61-73.

Kintzer, F. C., Jensen, A. M. & Hensen, J. S. (1969). The multi-institution junior college district. *American Association of Junior Colleges Monograph Series* (from ERIC Clearinghouse for junior college information).

Large ovation given new shrine member. (1976, November 4). *Stockton Record.* 22.

Lynes, R. (1966, November). How good are the junior colleges? *Harper's Magazine.* 18-26.

Mayhew, L. B. (1966, November 15). So they say about higher education, *AHE College & University Bulletin, 19.* 3.

New JTC Facility named for Priest.(1987, May). *Intercom.* 1.

Oppenheimer, E. and Porterfield, B. (1976). "Education" by Bill J. Priest, *The Book of Dallas.* Garden City, New York: Doubleday & Company.

Parsons, C. (1966, October 29). Is teaching an art? Is it a skill? Is it definable? *Christian Science Monitor.* 8.

Poised for greatness. (1965, December 20). *Dallas Morning News.* 4D.

Priest: Education in the middle of the turbulence. (1980, October 7). *Flair, The Newsmagazine of Mountain View College,* 6.

Priest resigns from Los Rios. (1965, August 8). *The Sacramento Union.* 2D.

Priest Selected for Shrine. (1976, October 26). *Stocton Record.* 12

Retiring chancellor reflects on DCCCD. (1980, September 16). *The Mesquite Daily News.* 2.

Shepicka, L. (1965, August 5). First President selected for junior college. *Dallas Morning News.* 3A.

Smith, K. B. (1966). Crossroads in Texas. *Junior Colleges: 20 States.* Washington, D.C.: American Association of Junior Colleges.

Stutz, Terrance. Community Colleges' time has come, ex-official says. (1981, January 4). *The Dallas Morning News.* 35A, 37A.

Tyler, H. T. (1966). Full partners in California's higher education. *Junior Colleges: 20 States.* Washington, D.C.: American Association of Junior Colleges.

United States Congressional Senate Record. (1972, March 22). Educational Opportunities for War Veterans. S4503.

Wilson, M. (1965, August 27). Mrs. Priest seeks new home. *Dallas Times Herald*, 1B.

Wright, J. (1978, April 21). Seventh campus. *Dallas Morning News*. 4D.

Torricelli, R., and A. Cavroll, eds. (1999) *In Our Own Words*. (April 12, 1945) Radio address on the death of Roosevelt & (August 6, 1945) Radio address on the bombing of Hiroshima. New York: Kodnsha International.

Unpublished Sources

Board of Trustees. (1965, August 4). Minutes of meeting, Dallas County Junior College District. District Offices, Dallas, Texas.

Board of Trustees. (1965, November 2). Minutes of meeting, Dallas County Junior College District, District Offices, Dallas, Texas.

Dallas County Community College District, catalog. (1980).

Dallas County Community College District, Public Information Office, (1980). Biographical information on Dr. Bill J. Priest

Dallas County Community College District. Brookhaven College Catalog. (1994).

Faculty Council. (1992, October 2). Minutes of meeting, Dallas County Community College District. District Offices, Dallas, Texas.

Faculty Council. (1992, November 16). Minutes of meeting, Dallas County Community College District. District Offices, Dallas, Texas.

Gibbons, H. E. (1975). *The Historical Development of the Dallas County Community College District: A Study of a Multi-College District.* Unpublished doctoral dissertation, University of Oklahoma, Norman, Oklahoma.

Holt, H. D. (1970). *An Interpretive Analysis of the Developmental Planning of Mountain View College, Dallas, Texas.* Unpublished dissertation, University of Texas, Austin, Texas.

Neal, J. F. (1990). *The History of the Center for Telecommunications of the Dallas Community College District.* Unpublished doctoral dissertation, University of North Texas, Denton Texas.

Newport, D. (Producer and interviewer). (1981). *A Program In Community College Leadership: An Interview With Bill J. Priest* [video] Irving, Texas: North Lake College.

Priest, B. J. (1965, August). To the people of Dallas. Statement in press kit sent to the media. (Available in Bill Priest's private files).

Priest, B. J. (1967, May). Vocational and technical education in Texas. Remarks made to House Education Committee, Texas Legislature.

Austin, Texas. (Available in Bill Priest's private files).

Priest, B. J. (1980, July 8). Request for retirement presented to Dallas County Community College Board of Trustees. (Available in Bill Priest's private files).

Priest, B. J. (1981, January 16). Retirement Bash Comments. Presented at DCCCD Conference Day, Richardson, Texas. (Available in Bill Priest's private files).

Randolph, W. L. (1974). *An Interpretive Analysis of the Political Process Involved in the Establishment and Development of the Dallas County Community College District: 1964-1974.* Unpublished doctoral dissertation, University of North Texas, Denton, Texas.

Whitson, J. R. (Producer & Interviewer) (1980). *Point of View: An Interview with Patty Powell.* [television program] Fort Worth: KTVT.

Williams, J. D. (1968). *Major Educational Innovation: A Conceptual Model and A Case-Study Analysis of the Establishment of the Dallas County Junior College.* Unpublished dissertation. University of Texas, Austin, Texas.

Personal Interviews

Blackshear, R. (June 25, 1994). Instructor, El Centro College. Personal telephone interview with the author. Blackshear's home, Heath, Texas.

Campbell, R. (March 23, 1995). District Publication Specialist, Dallas County Community College District. Personal interview with author, Dallas County Community College District Office, Dallas, Texas.

Creamer, D. (November 4, 1994). Dean of Educational and Student Services, Virginia Polytechnic Institute and State University. Personal electronic mail interview with the author. Virginia Polytechnic Institute and State University, Blackburg, Virginia.

Eggleston, K. (February 8, 1995). District Coordinator of ADN Nursing Program, El Centro College. Personal interview with author, El Centro College, Dallas, Texas.

Flint, J. (December 6, 1994). Professor and coordinator, ADN Program Brookhaven College. Personal interview with the author. Brookhaven College, Farmers Branch, Texas.

Flint, J. (November, 2002). Executive Dean, Health and Human Service Division, Brookhaven College. Personal interview with the author, Brookhaven College, Farmers Branch, Texas.

Fulton, P. (November 3, 1994). Former chancellor of Oakland Community College, Michigan; she is currently an assistant professor at the

University of North Texas. Personal telephone interview with the author. Fulton's home, Bloomfield Hills, Michigan.

Fulton, S. (March 20, 1995). Professor of Electronics Technology, Mountain View College. Personal interview with the author, Mountain View College, Dallas, Texas.

Holt, D. (July 28, 1994). Chancellor Emeritus, Mira Costa College, Oceanside, California. Personal interview with the author. Radisson Inn, Amarillo, Texas.

LeCroy, R. J. (July 19, 1994). President, Dallas Citizen Council. Personal interview with the author. Dallas Citizen Council Office, Dallas, Texas.

Mittlestet, S. (October 20, 1994). President of Richland College. Personal interview with the author. Richland College, Richardson, Texas.

O'Banion, T. (March 24, 1995). President of League for Innovation. Personal telephone interview with author, League for Innovation Office, Mission Viejo, California.

Parnell, D. (March 28, 1995). Professor of Higher Education, Oregon State University. Personal telephone interview with author, Oregon State University, Oregon.

Priest, B. J. (July 5, 1994). Chancellor Emeritus of the Dallas County Community College District. Personal interview with the author. Richland College, Richardson, Texas.

Priest, B. J. (August 2, 1994). Chancellor Emeritus of the Dallas County Community College District. Personal interview with the author. Priest's home, Dallas, Texas.

Priest, B. J. (September 7, 1994). Chancellor Emeritus of the Dallas County Community College District. Personal interview with the author. Richland College, Richardson, Texas.

Priest, B. J. (October 26, 1994). Chancellor Emeritus of the Dallas County Community College District. Personal interview with the author. Priest's home, Dallas, Texas.

Priest, B. J. (October 18, November 21, December 18, 2002) Chancellor Emeritus of the Dallas County Community College District. Personal interview with the author. Priest's home, Dallas, Texas.

Rippey, D. (July 21, 1994). Retired professor, Community College Leadership Program, University of Texas, Austin, Texas. Personal interview with the author. Rippey's home, Austin, Texas.

Rippey, G. (July 21, 1994). Retired Dean of the Rio Grande Campus, Austin Community College, Austin, Texas. Personal interview with the author. Rippey's home, Austin, Texas.

Robinson, C. (August 26, 1994). Director of Public Information, Dallas County Community College District. Personal interview with the author. Crockett's Restaurant, Dallas, Texas.

Timmerman, L. (August 7, 2002). Vice President of Institutional Advancement, Navarro Community College. Personal interview with the author in her office at Navarro Community College, Corsicana, Texas.

Quinn, P. (October 4, 1994). Vice president of the LeCroy Center for Telecommunications. Personal interview with the author. LeCroy Center for Telecommunications, Richardson, Texas.

Weaver, G. (March 9, 1995). Professor of Biology, Eastfiled College. Personal interview with author, Eastfield College, Mesquite, Texas.

Index

164 • Index